In fond memory of Brenda Montgomery
1950 – 2012

You Are Greatly Missed

The Way We Were

Essays & Prose Poetry
by Brenda Montgomery

Winter Goose Publishing

Winter Goose Publishing
2701 Del Paso Road, 130-92
Sacramento, CA 95835

www.wintergoosepublishing.com
Contact Information: info@wintergoosepublishing.com

The Way We Were

COPYRIGHT © 2013 by Brenda Montgomery

ISBN: 978-0-9894792-8-8

First Edition, November 2013

Cover Painting by Brenda Montgomery
Cover Art by Winter Goose Publishing
Typesetting by Odyssey Books

Published in the United States of America

I am forever grateful to my maker for giving me the talent
and creative gift to write

I thank my children for enhancing my life with motherhood
My family for being part of the whole
My sisters for listening
My teachers for believing

A special thank you to Kathy for the early edits,
and for "everything," my dearest friend Rick,
and to all of those who have crossed my path

Foreword

Too soon did I meet and lose my friend, Brenda Montgomery. She was a beautiful whirlwind through my life and will be deeply missed.

It was January, 2012. I was holding my first *Inspiring Words* poetry series in my fairly new hometown in California. The local library had blessed us with a wonderful room with hopes we would stir up some locals. In walks Brenda, the first one to get there. She had a nervous smile on her face and reluctantly approached me to discuss her writing.

Brenda went into her past and was honest about her present. She brought up the inspiration of her childhood, and her children. Her hands shook as she spoke. There was something brutally honest about her that instantly intrigued me. Honest writing had always attracted me and I was nervous but excited to hear Brenda read during our open mic portion of the evening.

If anyone's ever attended an open mic night, you will understand my nervousness. You get a variety of people and you just never know what will happen.

Something I explained to Brenda's family at her funeral was how she reminded me that day to not assume anything. When she got up to read she melted my heart. Her words were mysterious, healing, and molded in truth. I was surprised by her beauty and from that day on, I loved Brenda.

She attended every event with hopes that one day she would publish and be featured. I'm honored to be able to assist her with one of those dreams before she passed. She deserved that dream to be fulfilled. Her words move me and I know they will move you, too.

I miss you, my friend.

Jessica Kristie
Award Winning Author, Poet, and Advocate

Contents

Welcome Home

I'm not likely to forget when I was five years old. That was the year I got my first new bike, but most important, it was the year my youngest sister was born. It was 1955 and we lived on Sherman Street in Phoenix, Arizona, in a little court, as my mother called it. There were six look-a-like units and Mom said we would move to a bigger place as soon as the baby was born. I thought we were very lucky as we were the only people I knew of who were getting a new baby. It was like getting a present.

While my dad and my sister Wilma, who was a year younger than me, went to the hospital to bring Mom and the baby home, Richie, who was three years old, and I waited at a neighbor's house for their return. It helped to pass the time, as we could hardly wait.

Lucky for us, my grandma—Mom's mom—came to our house to help out. Mom said Granny would stay for three months. Granny was making dinner and said she would come and get us when Mom came home. Mom had been gone for about four or five days and it was the longest time I can ever remember being away from her.

While we waited at the neighbor's house, Richie and I were trying to get coconut out of the hard shell. After tasting the coconut, we decided we didn't like it. It tasted strange and crunchy like raw turnips that I tasted once before when Mom cooked them. We sipped the coconut juice, that the neighbor said was milk, and we didn't like that either. But the neighbors were nice, we were having fun, and it helped us to wait.

"You kids excited?" he asked.

"Yep, I'm gonna help Mom with the baby. They named her Shirley."

"I bet you'll be Mom's little helper," he said.

Finally, Granny came to get us. "Come on kids, your mother is home and supper is almost ready." Granny thanked the neighbors and we took off running as fast as we could. Granny was not as fast as us kids and she didn't run with those big, black square-heeled shoes that tied. Her apron was dusty with flour.

We practically fell through the front door. Shirley was so tiny. I had dolls bigger than her. She was asleep and wrapped tight in a blanket. Mom said that was why they called it a security blanket. The baby felt secure and not wide open. Her little hand was sticking out of the blanket and it was tiny, too. Mom said we could touch her hand if we washed up first. Granny pulled bread out of the oven and said it was dinner time, but we were too excited to eat.

When I looked at Mom, it seemed like it had been a long, long time since we'd seen her. We three kids stood beside her. She said she missed us. In a white dress with little blue flowers she was sitting in a kitchen chair holding the baby. She looked pretty and soft, but tired. Even though Granny was happy, she said no more babies.

Mom went into the bedroom to lie down and as she got up I followed behind her. The quilt had been turned back and the sheets were crispy white. Granny and Dad loved doing things for Mom and they loved to work. I thought how lucky Mom was to have all of us. But I was very disappointed at Mom going to bed. Everything happened so quickly and I missed her. Granny called from the kitchen that it was time to eat.

We kids gathered around the table to our favorite spots. I heard Mom laughing at something Dad had said. I was excited again. But while Mom was gone, Granny told Dad off about something. Granny was usually right and I wondered if and when she would tell Mom.

I knew all was well, when Mom said she'd get up. Dad came into the warm kitchen and called Granny, Granny. He looked happy. Mom came to the table with baby Shirley. I wondered with all the commotion with the baby and all, would I still get my bike for Christmas.

Song of Words

Growing up during the fifties and sixties, story time was just as much a part of school life and daily activities as spelling, ant farms, and lunch. Story time was like someone gave us a gift. The stories were like winding down a lone country road and we kids were along for the ride. After the day's reading, if I saw the teacher on the playground, I would run up and ask her, "What happens next?" She'd say, "I'm not going to tell you, you'll have to wait for tomorrow and see." I would anxiously wait, hardly letting a word go, until the following day. When she announced that it was story time, I knew a different world would come to life right there in the classroom. We kids got to live it.

Some of my first memories were the printed word at story time, in a room that smelled like clay and books. We gathered in a circle and sat Indian style on a rug for half an hour without moving. Even though I was shy and usually sat in the back, I'd sit in the front only inches away from the teacher so I wouldn't miss a word she said. Mrs. Black, in third grade, said I was like a little mouse. We kids absorbed a kind of magic when her words came to life.

When the teacher read to us I could imagine myself a castaway, a hero, a fisherman, a king, or a young kid flying a real airplane. Right away I learned Mother Goose liked kids and things I'd never heard of before. We giggled when little Jack Horner stuck his thumb in a pie and pulled out a plum, and when Mary's lamb followed her to school. We kids could have done all of that, but we never did and that made it special. It was truly magic.

Then as the years passed, the circle vanished along with the familiar smells of childhood and the years of make believe. Instead, we read Shakespeare's *Romeo and Juliet* and outlined The Constitution. However, my own storytelling was about to take on some real tall, tall tales. In real life it was called lying.

From a young age I always told my mom true encounters about things from school or play. But the summer after eighth grade, when we moved from Arizona to California, I found that the truth hurt. I missed my friends, our home, familiar stomping grounds, and just everything about Arizona.

Mainly, the move left my friend Caryl to continue on to South Mountain High without me. The move placed me at Woodland High alone, even a stranger to myself as I learned how to start over and where I stood in a new location. Caryl and I wrote letters to each other. She wrote that some kids were asking about me, which made me homesick for Phoenix even more.

My sister Wilma was at Harriett Lee and would not join me for a year in September. I didn't know a living soul, except Ken, who lived across the street from where we were staying with friends until we found our own house. He was our tetherball friend and we played all summer in his front yard. I was grateful for the friendship. But once school started I hardly ever saw him.

Back in Phoenix we had a television show that was filmed in San Francisco called *Where the Action Is*. It was about surfing and teens on the beach. Because my loneliness grew, to dodge it, my letters grew. They were really, really big letters. I said to myself, San Francisco is only eighty miles from where we live so I'd better make the action happen like the name of the show.

So I spent a lot of time writing and lying to my friend Caryl. Sometimes the letters came back for more postage due or she paid the extra postage. The letters were ten pages or so. My attempt was to make the letters as interesting as the stories I had heard in grade school. When I was out of things to say, instead of ending the letters, I made things up. My mother never suspected that I was lying.

According to my letters I was a surfer, I saw all the movie stars, and flew to San Francisco to have lunch. I flew to Hollywood to buy school clothes. I was the belle of the ball and the rose in every weed patch. It was just like grade school; it was great and I wasn't lonely. I was busy being famous or on adventure. My letters grew from the transition. In fact, the letters were my transition. They helped me over a hump. I always had them to look forward to and it was great to have a friend who thought I was doing so well. It was great just having a friend.

Then, as time went on, Caryl and I started talking on the phone for a few minutes. She said that she was going to come and visit me. Her mom said she could. I had told some big lies and now I would have to face them. I was not belle of the ball, I bought my clothes at the local shopping center at JCPenney, and I'd never been to Hollywood or surfed. In fact I was afraid of the ocean and I'd probably get lost in Hollywood.

So I called Caryl and admitted my lies. She let me off easy and laughed at my tall tales. I suppose that's what friends do. I went easy on myself and told the truth from then on.

On my behalf, I found comfort recalling my great aunt Dolly's dress that had little brown flowers on it, and it was okay even though I'd never seen brown flowers before. And in grade school we had animals that talked and a cow that jumped over the moon. All was okay. The truth then is the same truth today. Grade school never ends and our life is story after story.

Our Own Backyard

For the fourteen years we lived in Phoenix, Arizona, my mother's anemia was too bothersome for the dry heat of summer, and my father's job closed for three months each year. So Mom and Dad would pack up the '55 Ford and the highway was our passage of escape and new adventures. We would return to Phoenix when the blistering summer was over.

Mom packed the back seat and floor board in order to make a double-size bed in the back of the car for me, my two younger sisters, and my brother. We had plenty of room to stretch out and we had a grand view in the front, on the sides, and behind us. We had soft quilts and fluffy pillows, and the promise of a colorful summer away from our everyday happenings. It was not uncommon to go to sleep in one state and wake up in another. It was always like getting a surprise. At night we kids would go to sleep in Arizona, somewhere down the road, and wake up in New Mexico or Texas, and we once traveled to Michigan.

We kids made faces and shapes from the clouds, caught rain drops as they hit the windows, and we saw for the first time, no matter how often our trips, new horizons from the eyes of make believe and anticipation.

One of Mom's requirements was that we stop frequently to stretch and see what there was to see. We stopped at rest stops so we could use the outdoor water to brush our teeth, wash up, and change our clothes.

Often, we bought things from little markets to make lunch, and Mom would pick out a large tree to eat under. Many times, Mom picked out a big cottonwood tree with the little fuzzy things floating in the air that looked as if it were snowing. A few times she and Dad made breakfast at rest stops in the wide open spaces. Always, there was some kind of treasure at those spots. We kids found unusual rocks, twisted wood, wild flowers, and sometimes signs that someone had been there before us.

During the fifties, at a little court where we lived for the summer, we kids chased wild cats, thinking we could keep one if we tamed it. We finally realized it was too hard to catch wild things, gave up the idea, and observed from afar.

In Albuquerque, we discovered the potato bug called Child of the Earth. It was the scariest bug we kids had ever seen, and for a couple of days we did not venture past the front porch. We saw a hair from a horse's tail turn into a thin black snake and swim away in a little clear canal in Farmington; or at least we thought we did. Also, in Albuquerque, we kids climbed crab apple and apricot trees in early morning and played in dry, golden, sand bottom canals. Morning smelled rich and full of things growing in moist dirt, and smelled of new things coming, as we were in full celebration. Our spirits were enriched, as we kids ran from street to street hunting out new things to see. We ran to the beat of adventure with kids who were as free as we were for summer play.

In Prescott, Arizona, we lived in a little cabin in the woods one summer, and our cousin, Ronnie, let us kids hold his pet baby bear in our cradled arms. We walked through a house that was left as it was when a woman had walked to the store to get milk for her kids and was hit and killed by a car. We touched her things and I felt her ghost. I was saddened for her children's loss.

Our trips were endless. We threw little rocks over the cliffs of the Grand Canyon to see who could throw the furthest; swam in the Colorado and Verde Rivers, reservoirs; and fished at all the man-made lakes. We visited reservations: ancient Indian ruins and cliff dwellings, botanical gardens, ghost towns. We climbed the Gila Bend Mountains, saw oil wells, jack rabbits, roadrunners, sidewinders, and the Petrified Forest.

While on the road we stopped at all-night cafes and I was surprised at how many adults liked kids who had just awakened, hungry and thirsty with hair sticking up, shoes on the wrong feet and pants twisted. The customers, sitting at the counter, always gave us kids nickels for penny candy as we stood in a tasseled look while on the road trip in the middle of nowhere.

Then, at the end of summer, it was time to go back home to Phoenix. It was time to let it all go and say goodbye to a chunk of the world. Reluctantly, we gave up new acquaintances, new friends never to see again, old play grounds, and we traded wishful thinking for gathered treasures. But, we felt lucky for having parents who gave us a piece and a glimpse of the world. Our summers were rich with fruit in our own backyards in the USA, a home that left imprints, footsteps, and impressions for all time. .

The Canal

On a blistering-hot Phoenix summer morning in 1955, Mom was getting her hair pin-curled by a neighbor while the two of them visited and drank iced tea. Mom never visited with anyone without sharing tea. It was a friendly announcement that she had time to visit and was taking a break from her home duties, kids, and whatever else popped up. It meant free time and we kids got a break from chores that could last throughout the entire day. We kids got tea also, just not as much as the adults.

Mom's tea always looked pretty and refreshing in the mason jars she used instead of glasses. She said the jars kept the tea colder for a longer period of time and the ice took longer to melt. She bought the ice block from the ice company and used a pick to chop it up. She called it crystal ice and said it was from spring water. We could see all the way through the ice and it looked like the diamond in Mom's wedding ring. The ice block was put in Dad's aluminum ice chest she kept in the kitchen, and we had tea every day. We kids weren't allowed to touch the pick, it was too sharp and Mom was always one to watch her kids closely. Everyone said how well behaved we were and she said she could take us anywhere because we were so good. They also commented on how our hair always shone.

On this particular morning, my brother Ritchie and I were playing in the courtyard outside our front door. Ritchie was only three and I was six. Dad said our house was called a unit because it was too small to be called a house. There were others identical to ours that surrounded the courtyard. I don't recall how Ritchie and I ended up at the canal that Mom had warned us about. We must have wandered down or perhaps wanted to get a closer look at running water. But we knew it was off limits to us.

A large wooden plank bridge went from the road across the canal to the graveled courtyard. The water was a few inches below the bridge and we kids always looked out the car windows, as we drove across to try and see how deep it was and if there were fish big enough to eat you.

On this day, we broke a rule that was almost deadly to my little brother. There we were standing at the edge of the canal. There were other kids from the courtyard there. We were staring down at the muddy water. In an instant, without any kind of a warning, Ritchie fell in, went under water, and never came up. We kids waited as we all jumped up and down in our disbelief. The water was moving, but calm, and we kids became silent as we waited for some sign that he would come up out of it. I knew not to wait any longer and took off running across the courtyard to get Mom. My legs were running as fast as they could and I was screaming and calling for Mom. All I could see was the moving water.

Mom and the neighbor lady took off running towards the canal across the courtyard. I was gonna be in so much trouble. Mom was running as fast as her bare feet would carry her. Other neighbors came running to see what the commotion was all about.

The neighbor, whose name I can't remember, jumped in the canal and went under the water. He came up a few times without my brother. Mom was crying and her face was white and crunched up. She was trying to get into the canal and the man told her to stay on the bank—it wasn't safe. Everything happened so fast. Then the man swam under the bridge. We waited as everything then became very slow. I didn't care if I got spanked or not; I just wanted my little brother to be all right.

After a long while, the neighbor man surfaced holding my brother. Ritchie was crying and everyone on the bank of the canal was cheering and clapping. Mom was crying even harder now. He handed Ritchie to my mom and said "Here's your baby." The back of Ritchie's brown plaid shirt was all torn and the neighbor man said Ritchie's shirt got hung up on a nail under the bridge. He said the nail probably saved him. He said all the kids needed a few swats for coming to the canal.

Mom carried Ritchie to our house and I followed behind them. In her wet dress, bare feet, and partially curled hair, she turned to me and said I'd done a good job coming to get her, but not ever to let her see me at the canal again. "Your brother almost didn't make it out alive," she added.

I noticed, probably for the first time, how little Ritchie was and how I was much bigger. I didn't get spanked; Mom was too thrilled and said she should have been watching us better.

She took us in, bathed us, fed us, and put us down for a nap. After that we couldn't play much beyond our doorstep. When Dad came home from work, Ritchie sat on his lap. I can never ever remember living next to a canal after that.

Odessa

In the fifties, Dad said Odessa, Texas, was located at the end of the earth. Mom corrected him and said it was the end of the earth. We kids believed it because our parents said so. Dad said Odessa wasn't as pretty and green as Houston where he had been born. His relatives lived in Odessa and our visits there were usually short. Once we tried living there, but we went back to Phoenix; Dad and Mom said Dad's family was a little too rowdy for us.

I can remember Aunt Ruth, Dad's older sister, believed in fighting. She taught her three girls to fight and Mom said they brawled like wild boys. Many times when we girls were sent to the corner store for something Aunt Ruth needed, my cousins would get into fights with other kids. The other kids always got the worst end of the fight. Most often, my cousins instigated the encounters. My sister Wilma and I were too peaceful to join in. Those poor kids fought for their lives. We always tried to stop them, but my cousins were mean hellions. Mom would usually say my sister and I could never go to the store again with them.

When we girls arrived back at my aunt's house, Aunt Ruth would hear the story from my cousins and she'd clap her hands and laugh and say, "They know not to mess with you girls; you'll lick 'em every time." Then she'd say, "I'm glad you girls whooped 'em."

Mom always said, "My kids better not be fighting." In fact, if my sister and I would have fought, and we didn't know how, we would have gotten a spanking, and if my cousins didn't fight, they would get a spanking. According to Aunt Ruth it was always the other kids' fault. Dad just said we lived on the other side of the tracks, and Mom said they didn't know any better. A few times my oldest cousin Ruby's temper was unleashed on me and Dad ended our visit and we packed up and went home to Phoenix. Mom and Dad talked about how unruly they were. I always felt sorry for my dad for being related to such an ornery group of people, or bunch, as my mom called them.

Mom said to us kids, "Your dad is the best one out of the whole clan."

Mom and Dad loved to sit a talk with one another and there was calmness about both of them. Dad was always full of something that had happened. No matter how serious the situation in the story, he found humor and lightness in the problems. He played the guitar or piano and sang his heart out to the music of Hank Williams, Ernest Tub, Jim Reeves, and all those who contributed to the country western tunes of day-to-day life. Even though we went to church on Sundays, at our house, in our kitchen, we kids heard all about honky-tonk blues, cheatin' hearts, crawfish pie, lost loves, and all kinds of things that happened for the sake of winning and in losing. Like poetry, even the saddest of songs had a beauty, and we all listened even if we were busy in another room. If Dad was not telling a story, he picked up his guitar and sang to all of us. One thing was certain, neither Mom nor Dad liked Odessa.

The first time I saw a field of oil wells I lost my breath. The smell was unlike any other smell—one of a kind. It smelled like an old car or an old shoe. Mom said it smelled like hot tar that roofers used. The oil rigs looked like they were growing right out of the ground like jet-black grasshoppers or big black monsters. There were hundreds with big arms that went up and down; it was the most beautiful, yet ugliest, sight I'd ever seen.

They were so different from our fields of Japanese gardens in Phoenix, with sweet peas growing in fields as far as one could see, taller than our heads in every Easter color that ever was. The smell of the oil field worked its way up the nostrils and down to the middle of the stomach until all the air smelled like that. My dad said it was the smell of money. Those giant monster-looking grasshoppers sprouted right out of the dirt. In fact, most of Odessa was sitting in the dirt and sand. When the dry wind blew it was hard to see. The dirt and sand got into our eyes and Mom took a washcloth to our faces constantly.

Somehow, fond memories survived the trips like the time we fed the chickens, and when we picked tomatoes for dinner from Aunt Ruth's garden. How happy we kids were when Mom told Aunt Ruth we did not like black-eyed peas, and we didn't have to eat those dusty things. A visit to Odessa was when we got our pixie shoes. They looked like ballet slippers and had little gold coins on them that jingled when we walked. Mom said for sure we looked like gypsies. But the best time we ever had was when my grandpa, Dad's dad, George, asked my cousin Ruby and me to work at his fruit stand. He had to go around the countryside and to New Mexico to get fresh fruit. Ruby was about sixteen and I was about twelve or thirteen. Grandpa said he'd be gone four days, our parents would keep an eye on us, we could eat all the fruit we wanted, and he'd pay us.

He had peaches, watermelon, honey dew, cantaloupe, apples, oranges, and lots of onions. We were in produce heaven. Mom, Dad and Aunt Ruth picked us girls up at the end of the day, after checking on us mid-day. Grandpa had a little trailer at the fruit stand that he lived out of when he sold fruit. It had a large blue tarp and frame that covered the fruit from the scorching sun. We sat on little canvas stools outside the trailer door in the shade until some big oversized car pulled up in the dust, so the occupants could buy Grandpa's fruit. Then we would jump to our feet and do our jobs. We felt pretty grown up and our parents trusted us with the freedom.

The fruit stand sat back away from the busy highway. The two roads crossed and there was a lot of non-stop traffic. Grandpa said it was the best corner spot in Odessa. One lady buying onions said we were doing a good job and that we looked cute. We gave her free peaches. Well, we did so well selling fruit we decided to take soda breaks, a lot of soda breaks, soda breaks that did not belong to us. We drank the sodas and laughed at our calamity of being our own boss.

Over a period of four days we took seven dollars of Grandpa's change to buy sodas. We'd sell fruit and run and buy more soda. The sodas were the prize. My cousin gave me the money as she was the one in charge, and I did the running and buying across the highway. I had to be careful crossing the road; I was too young to do that but I did it anyway. It only seemed like change at the time, but as time went on it grew into dollars. We hid the bottles out behind the trailer. Some of the bottles we cashed back in for deposit money to buy more sodas. I had orange Crush and Ruby had grape or strawberry. They were freezing cold in the hot day around us. After a while the man at the gas station said he'd have to restock the soda box and he laughed. Then we started to worry.

The smell of the fruit stand had a sweet musty smell. I could smell the dirt field that the melons grew in and it reminded me of the khaki clothes Grandpa wore. I could even smell his hat. We plugged melons for the customers and ate some of the melons we'd plugged. They were sweet and full of juice, and didn't taste anything like the smell of the dirt field. The melons tasted rich with summer.

When business was slow I went into Grandpas trailer and cleaned it spotless. The sink was scratched and stained so I painted it black with some paint I'd found on a shelf. I thought if we had black sinks they'd be beautiful and fancy enough for a magazine.

Then Grandpa came back and was pleased with the job we had done. He was especially happy about his clean trailer. But when he saw the black sink he said, "Don't that beat all." Even though he didn't look or act pleased, I could almost see a smile on his face. I could tell in his eyes he wanted to laugh, but he didn't. When Mom and Dad picked us up, he took them in the trailer. I knew he was going to show them the black sink. We girls were worried about the sodas and the money but it was too late. Dad asked me what in the world was I thinking to paint the sink black. I said I thought it would be pretty. He shook his head. I had to scrape the paint off of the sink, but I had not gotten into trouble—yet.

The next day, Grandpa came to tell our parents that he found twenty pop bottles behind his trailer, and he figured we had drunk some of his profits. We had to give back some of the money he had paid us for working. Ruby got spanked; she was the one in charge and the oldest. I felt terrible and sick. Not because we were caught, but because we had stolen Grandpa's money. We weren't that cute or comical, or independent or grown up after all. I learned about freedom and how we all have to answer to someone, especially to ourselves at all times.

To this day, I cannot look at an oil well without thinking of my mom and my dad, his family, our visits to Odessa, the guitar, and the country singers that Dad said were spit out of Bakersfield in the forties and fifties like a hail storm. Every once in a while I have a memory of Odessa's simple days and something we loved to hate; and when I visit an outdoor fruit stand I behave myself. I can't help but wonder if Grandpa would like the black sinks that are as common as orange Crush on a hot summer's day.

Moving

When we were kids, Mom loved to move and Dad went along with her wishes. Moving was something I liked, but at the same time something I didn't like. It was continuous as I was growing up. The adventure of getting a new house was exciting, but it meant that we would also get a new neighborhood with strangers and we were always the new kids in school. However, I must say that during the summer, we kids liked the adventure of new places to explore with newly made friends, but new schools were scary.

Teachers would say, time and time again, "Class, we have a new student." All eyes would be on me as I stood awkwardly in front of the classroom while the kids looked, stared, and summed me up. My sister Wilma said we moved thirteen times in thirteen years. It may sound as if my parents were a bit on the dysfunctional side, but the truth was, Mom just loved moving and we kids loved the adventure. The new school was the only exception that did not make us happy. I found just about the time the other kids finally accepted me, a shy, awkward, slinky, freckle faced girl, it was time to move again. As much as I loved my mother, she was at fault.

In second grade, at Murphy Grade School, I cried a lot. I arrived the week of Valentine's Day. How could I put the Valentine's cards in the bags of people I didn't even know, or even know who they were? The cards said things like *best friends*, *best teacher*, and *I love you*. I was embarrassed, and seemed so out of place. I hardly got any cards from anyone. Kids were busy giving cards to their friends or favorite people. They didn't know me either.

Again, tears came when I lost my lunch token. Teachers were strict then and my teacher said it was my responsibility to hang onto the token. I cried harder. A few weeks after that, the lunch duty teacher made me eat the macaroni and cheese from the lunch menu, even though it made me sick. I threw it up in front of the whole school and felt that I had been turned inside out. I didn't know if I could ever live again in front of my classmates. Being new was always hard for me. Mom was always coming to school on my behalf.

Sometimes I was a handful for my teachers. I didn't do well under stern authority. Even though I was shy, all knew when I was upset. Tears just kind of exploded from me when something really bothered me. I felt like a big baby and I wanted to be home with my mom in familiar surroundings. I would ask to call my mom, sometimes I demanded it and a few times I just ran home. The beginnings were usually dreadful.

Finally, we settled down when I was in the seventh and eighth grade. My shyness and awkwardness had vanished. I had a few friends who actually carried over from the sixth grade. It was so wonderful knowing I would go to high school with kids I knew.

Then it happened again. Mom and Dad decided to move to Woodland, California, where we had visited friends of the family a few summers earlier. Their friends said Woodland was a good place to raise kids.

So, in the summer after eighth grade graduation, I said goodbye to my friends and to the idea that I would go to South Mountain High School. We moved to Woodland and once again, I was the new kid on the block, the transplant that no one had ever heard of, in a little clicky town, twenty miles from the capitol of California.

Mom and Dad packed up our '55 two-tone, peach Ford and pulled a trailer of household items behind it. Mom gave lots of things away. She and Dad packed the back seat and floorboard up level with the back of the front seats. Mom said we kids needed a place to stretch out on our trip. Plus we could fall asleep anytime we wanted to and be comfortable. Then she threw on a quilt and some pillows and, whamo, a full-size bed.

Before we left, Wilma and I called our friends to say goodbye and to get addresses so we could write letters. We swore we'd be friends forever. I cried all the way to California. But I didn't let Mom see me; I didn't want to spoil her joy of moving.

Driving away, we left the early Indians who had built their homes on the sides of mountains. We left the cactus, the desert, and the Sunday drives behind us. Mom said California would not be as hot, and we would have the beaches and the ocean. Plus, Woodland was smaller than Phoenix. Even though I was excited, I was sad that I would leave the friends I did have and doors would be shut forever again.

Leaving Arizona, lying on my back on the bed Mom made us, I could get a full view out the back window and see the sky. To this day, it remains imprinted in my memory. It was the most beautiful sky I'd ever seen. It was sharp blue with white puffy clouds that looked like giant cotton balls, and in some places, reminded me of spilt milk. The sky was so blue it looked similar to a swimming pool and I named it swimming pool blue. Later, I would come to know that it was due to atmosphere. All I knew then was that Arizona had the prettiest sky I'd ever witnessed and that's all there was to it.

I said goodbye to the beautiful city that had been our home for fourteen years. Goodbye to the eighth grade talent show when we won first place at pretending to be The Supremes and did our version of "Stop in the Name of Love." Goodbye to the runway for the homemade fashion show and the bravery of wearing black nylons on stage that everyone's mother in the audience whispered about; and goodbye to Gary, my eighth grade crush. No longer was I the scared little girl calling home to Mom. I had grown into my own comfort from a shy, awkward girl to what I was becoming. My sister Wilma, one year younger than me, was right behind me in growing to a time and age that left our self-consciousness behind.

My sister Wilma hated the move even more than I did. She cried too. She had been a star on the track team and the entire school loved her. Finally, we fit in. I told her, as new kids, we would just have to practice what we had learned. Our plan was that after her eighth grade, she would join me in high school. I promised her I'd be waiting and she said she would hurry up. She ended up graduating high school early because of her hard work. When she first started high school, we both knew that friends would come and go, but she and I would still be there for one another forever. And it didn't matter which sky we lived under or which desk we sat at or which state we lived in. We had each other, our baby sister, our brother, and our silly parents. We had learned a lot and I just knew there was something good about it all.

I now fly to Idaho to see my sisters. I usually can't wait to get there for our visits. Never do I compare the skies, and the trip is always an adventure like it was when we were growing up. We learned a lot. Even in our discomfort and sad times of letting go with each move, we learned a lot from our parents and I would never trade those times or wish it had been different. It was what it was, and we kids were the remnants of the good old days before time changed it all.

Who Am I

Up from the dusty streets of Bakersfield, California, five years after the end of World War II, in the breezy month of September, I was born. The year was 1950 and my mother's Oklahoma heritage and my father's Texas heritage never changed to the liberal attitudes with their move to California. Throughout my life, I would come to know that values, work, and love all went hand in hand. And during the fifties, they were woven into our lives from what our parents did for us, what we did for ourselves, and how our parents both worked in their separate roles.

In spite of the chores I grew up with, and my awkward shyness, I found my play and my joy in telling stories of whatever I saw or experienced in my small world in the hours I was away from home at school or at a neighbor's house. In doing so, I can remember my first memories of making my world bigger with my stories, and I could bring entertainment to my parents. My father also loved to tell stories, and I noticed how everyone listened and enjoyed his humor and his experiences. My mother was a reader and she read books with historical settings. Also, she was a good listener and our audience. She loved the tales I brought home from my day or from the corner store.

When I was seven, we were visiting my father's relatives somewhere in Texas, and my great aunt Dollie, after listening to me telling my mother about something from the kids outside, said to my mother, "She's probably going to be a writer." I didn't know what that meant, but her eyes and smile said it was something good. Mom said, "Well this is how we live with her, always a story."

As a teenager, my brother played the guitar, my sisters sang while my father played the guitar or piano, and my mother gave them her attention as the audience. I could not sing or dance, nor would I even attempt to, but I could write poetry and put on a play for my mother and her friends, as long as the audience was not too large. My siblings were always on stage when we had company and often the company would request my sisters to sing. I always felt like a tumbleweed because my poetry was written in some far corner of the house or backyard when I was alone. It seemed so small compared to what my siblings could do, and not anyone ever requested for me to read a poem. But, it made my mother happy, and I strived to have something all my own that I could do.

I always wondered if anyone had ever been to Bakersfield or even heard of it. I would come to know that my father's and mother's values on work most likely sprouted like the cotton and grapes in the stopping point of the depression, in an arid little corner of California.

Consequently, quite a few people had their lives meshed with mine and have helped me become the person I am today. My mother and father, a handful of teachers, and even strangers deserve to be honored for the person that I am and the person I am becoming. They taught me the basics of responsibility, work, and love being the foundation to inner happiness and balance. Above all, they taught me simplicity as being important to my personhood. I have been in the company of people who have dug ditches and cleaned toilets for a living, and people who were millionaires. I learned from both and am content with diversity and a wide range of people.

Even more important, my four children have brought me much joy and humor. They, too, have taught me many things. In addition, as a mother and wife, I learned and grew from the experience of being humble, nurturing, sensitive, empathetic, and grateful for all I had been a part of.

Then, entering college in the eighties was a first step toward venturing out of the tightly knit circle of mother and wife. I stumbled, I fell, I got up, I dropped out, I went back and finished my degree. My teachers were there with positive words and encouragement. Meshing the world of home and school was important to me, for yet another growth. It was time to move on in my life. It was no longer the fifties. It was the eighties and society, life, people, and mainly women had changed. It was my job as a person to change also. It was hard. I took everything I had learned in my life, whole pieces, broken pieces, and fit them into the new era. I learned that I had been many things and things I had not thought of yet.

Who am I? I am the person I want to be. I am the dusty roads of Bakersfield. I am the cotton and the grapes. It's all in the heart of who I am. The Montgomery family, my children the Christen family, in Woodland, another little corner in California, some have heard of us. We sing, we dance, we write, we paint, and we are a lively, comical clan. We are rich in spirit, simplicity, and nature oriented.

In as much, my life is still evolving and unfolding with delight. My children, also, are growing spiritually, and we have good friendships with one another. They are a compliment to their years. I owe them a lot with their good behavior and their help with our added work load with life.

Indeed, I went to college just as my parents came to California for a better life. And in my life and in my writing, I have evolved into something stronger and more in touch with myself and with others. I am part of the beginning, the middle, and the end in reference to my own story. Above all, I am an important figure in the lives of my family, and to my own experiences from education in the classroom to education on the streets. There is no place I'd rather be than in the here and now. Alone, I am one, with my family and others, I am many. I am inspired in this life.

Ever After

It was April of 1969, a year that would change my life for the next twenty years. I was just finishing up my senior year when I met George. A friend, Peggy, from high school, who was married, came over to my house with the purpose of asking me to go on a blind date with her husband's good friend. She said his name was George, he had been married for three years and was now divorced, just gotten out of Vietnam, and was five years older than me. While she told me about him, I saw stop signs right away. I knew my mom and dad would say no. When Peggy came to ask me to go on a date, my parents were not at home. I spoke for my parents as I saw flashing red lights. In addition, my parents would say they didn't even know him. I could just envision their reaction and it was not a good sight. They grew up in the dinosaur days when things were not as big. And this was too big for little ole me. So I sent her away knowing I had made the right decision for myself. My sister Wilma was proud of me and said, "They'd never let you go; he's been married before." I agreed.

Another consideration was that Wilma and I did not date that often. We had regular babysitting jobs and had even worked on the tomato harvester with our friends from school. In addition, we could only go out one day a week so we usually took our baby sister, Shirley, cruising down Main Street and around town or to a school function. We liked being home and our parents liked us home.

Besides that, there was my friend John, only a couple of years older than me, who I had been dating off and on since I was a junior in high school. We went steady for a while, but I broke it off because he had "two timed" me with a friend of mine. Kid stuff, in a grown up's world. I said no more going steady for me. I was too young to think of such things and my parents said so, also. Instead, I wrote John a poem titled

"Only friends." However, I did not want to lose his friendship. I always missed people who came and went from my life. He was a special friend to me. Then he was off to Vietnam, and he had asked me to marry him, but when I met him on his R & R in Hawaii, I declined, knowing I was too young.

So Peggy left my house, only to return a few days later. Mom and Dad were gone again. We saw Peggy from the street, getting out of her car and she looked hopeful and determined. I did a very non-grown up thing. Being the big girl I was, I ran and hid in my mom and dad's closet. Now, I was hopeful, hopeful that she'd just go away. I had tried to tell her I didn't want to date a divorced man, but she had the problem of finding a date for her husband's friend, and didn't seem to take no for an answer.

After my sister Wilma told her I was not at home, Peggy left; and I came out of the closet. My sister and I laughed at our cleverness.

Once again, a few days passed and Peggy was on our doorstep. She was becoming a regular. I ran again and hid in the closet and my sister told her I was not home. I would have been braver and told her myself, but she was so persistent and didn't seem to hear the word *no*.

If only my mom knew what we were doing. She would never allow us to lie, or the foolishness of me hiding in the closet. I must have been eighteen going on five.

As time went on, I discovered Peggy was having a hard time finding a compatible date for their friend. She had her sights set on me and refused to give up. She came back a fourth time, and this time my mom was home and it would be a bit more serious.

Mom answered the door and Peggy asked for me. Mom invited her in. If there was a god, I didn't think he was there in our living room. We were face to face on a subject that didn't seem to go away. Again, Peggy asked me about the blind date and said she could not find anyone. She said she thought I'd like him and that he was a very nice guy. Immediately, Mom said, " We will have to ask her dad." Before I could say no, Peggy said, "Please Brenda, it will be fun." Mom said jokingly, "If she doesn't go, then I will." We laughed.

Little did my mom know this George character had been married then had gotten divorced. Peggy left that part out, as she told us information about him to lock in the plan with my mom. She said he had gone to Woodland High and graduated in 1965. He was born in Argentina, but his family came from Switzerland. He had lived in Woodland since he was nine years old. As my mom smiled I couldn't help but think maybe she should go out with him. I didn't want to be the bad guy so I went along with the conversation. I finally told myself that it would not be the end of the world. So right there in our living room I said, "Well, maybe I'll go if Dad says it is okay." Peggy was happy and said I'd like him.

After we talked it over with my dad, he said they'd have to meet him. He was to arrive one hour before the date. So the following Friday evening was set in stone and I was scared. A closet would not help me this time.

My sister and I had only been on one blind date. It was in San Francisco at my cousin Rose's. Wilma and I wore identical poke-a-dot pants with matching jackets. Hers was pink and mine was lavender. I wanted the pink set but she chose it first. I wished her date was my date and she wished mine was hers. Everyone was confused. My cousin thought we were funny. Nevertheless, we had a good time touring San Francisco and viewing our confused dates.

When Friday arrived, my nervousness from the week's anticipation was subsiding as the day arrived in full bloom, without question. I would be going out with a stranger, but viewed myself as one in the crowd after my own personal pep-talk. Mom chuckled and Dad was quiet. Wilma was full of joy and ran around the house like a fairy. She had previously started dating someone I had been seeing a few times and now probably felt a freedom that locked her in on her stolen festivities. I forgave her, a little.

Then there was my baby sister, Shirley, who followed me around as I was getting ready for my date. It seemed like she didn't want to miss a thing. And she didn't miss anything as she was under my feet, beside me and in my hair. I wore pink after settling on green and blue then back again. George and his friend Nick arrived on time.

After the introductions, they sat down and my dad, representing himself, went over some rules. I peeked around the corner and George looked older than the boys at school. He didn't look like my type, too grown up for me. I said to myself, it's just a date. I was glad I was still getting ready with the last touches so as not to witness the calamity of parents protecting a little queen. When Dad said I had to be home by ten thirty I was shocked. Then he said that I'd better return in the same manner I left in. I remember thinking *help, help, how will I ever live all this down*. It was worse than Dad coming into the dance at school to pick us up. Parents never beat around the bush.

To make matters worse, my baby sister Shirley went into the front room to announce that I was putting blush on my chest. I knew I'd get back at her later. I brushed the blush off and thought, *how will I ever survive this day?*

Finally, I swallowed hard and stepped out into the front room, to what I did not know then, my future. Dad agreed to let me stay out until eleven pm. By now I felt like a big baby instead of a little baby.

However, the date was fun. We went dancing to Davis at Mousy's and I saw kids from school. George was nice and polite. We continued to double date over the summer and my parents grew to like George. For a while, I did not tell George about John or John about George. I knew we were only friends so I didn't think it was that important. Well, it was not that simple. George was getting closer to me than what I realized, and probably me towards him. I just did not want to admit it.

Subsequently, John came home for a visit from the service and matters had to be addressed. One afternoon John and I went for a ride near Winters, twenty miles away. During our ride, I told him about George. I started to cry and cry. In my heart of hearts, I knew things would be changed forever. I didn't want our friendship to end. And I realized I did not have control over a lot of things. Life just could not be put in a perfect order and we do not always get our way with things. He said all was okay. And then asked me if we could still see each other and I said yes. But intuition told me I'd be put on the spot. George would not like it and would want me to see him only. I continued to cry because I knew one of the friendships would have to go. I'd have to let go.

John was so thoughtful and said I could drive his little MG yellow sports car. He said he'd leave it in my care when he went back to the service to complete his time. I said okay, knowing that nothing would be for certain.

Finally, I told George about John. And as I suspected, George said if I dated him I could not date John. I thought it over and over for a solution without giving up a friendship. There was not one. John and I stopped dating, but he came to my house for a few visits. And then, I let him go as our visits got further and further apart. He was my little friend who I would miss for years to come.

As time went on, George and I became closer, but he became late for our dates. A few times he didn't arrive at all. Even my mom said it's not fashionable to be late and that I should not see George for a while. But George would apologize and I didn't want to be so strict so I'd forgive him. One evening he sent his friend Don to tell me that he may stop seeing me. George told him that he was getting too serious about me. I guess it inflated my ego and I walked around feeling light footed for a while. Then reality hit hard. George and I had a date again, but he never showed up. I came back down to earth quickly. I called John.

I was sick of all the late times George finally would show up and the times he never came at all. I did not deserve that. So even though I had put John second, he said he was on his way over.

My mom and her friend Trisha were visiting and Mom said, "What if George is just late and they both come at the same time. What are you going to do then?" I made a childish decision and said, "I'll go with the first one that shows up." My upset caused the action I was creating. "John and I, we are going to the movies, I'm not going to date George," I said. Mom cheered me on and said George should not be late all the time and did not deserve my friendship. Mom and Trisha were laughing at my predicament. And it wasn't even my fault. It was no laughing matter. To read of it in a story was one thing and the drama was funny, but to be in the center of it all was quite another thing. In real life, my stomach hurt and there was nothing funny or cute about any of it. One thing was for certain, I was on the edge of myself and my decisions at the moment were made out of disappointment, hurt feelings, and losing a friendship. I was not being rational. I was surprised my mom let me make that decision. I suppose she thought I needed to learn from it. I had a pocket full of worry. It felt like the time I hid in my mom's closet.

Low and behold, as it happened before my eyes, with John on his way over, George pulled into our driveway first. Even though I felt like I should not go with him, I went anyway. Just as we were pulling away, John, in his little sports car pulled up and George turned the wheel towards John's car. Now, I was angry. I should have gotten out of the car, but I didn't. Poor John just drove past my house slowly. I felt like a rat. I thought the world of John.

I saw John a few times after that when he came to visit to say goodbye on his way to Oklahoma, back to the service. He was giving my sister Wilma a ride to Prescott, Arizona, to visit our grandmother. There was dust on the back of his car, and as one last silly thing to do, I wrote *just married* with my finger in the dust. I felt sad that the time was changed and gone like the wind—for all time. I think I must have been trying to make light of the moment and add some laughter to the seriousness of it all.

After John left, George presented me with an engagement ring and I, grown up or not, accepted it. I wore it like I'd worn John's class ring. But this was much bigger. I asked myself if I loved George and my answer was, I liked him a lot. However, I didn't know much about that grown up stuff or a darn thing about that kind of love. At nineteen I did not see rockets going off or sparks flying on the tail end of hearts. Mom said I was a late bloomer. I gave George the ring back a few times, only to accept it back, with an apology from him for being late; and my parents thought the world of George.

We were married October 11, 1969, in Davis, California. Our marriage would last nineteen years and seven months. It would bring to us four wonderful children and a piece of the rock. We had many years of day-to-day living, vacations, camping, boating, holidays, fixing up our different houses, and friendship. George stopped being late. Forty years later, we are still friends.

I saw John once over the twenty years at a little corner store. He had two of his children with him. They were as darling as mine were. Between us, things were forever different and somehow, forever the same.

Apology to First Born

Ernie, first of all let me say without you there would have been no family. Your father and I were a couple until you came along. Then we started doing family things like visiting relatives more often, taking lots of pictures, and special dinners at home on Sundays.

Can you forgive me for encouraging you to walk at five months and to talk at one month old? I had high hopes even as you slept. You were an example of our love.

You are not alone. Unlike their siblings, I have read that most first borns are prompted to start everything at an earlier age. We had the relatives believing it was the first time in history a child like you had ever been born. You could not do anything without your father and me saying, "Did you see that?" It was a wonder you didn't go blind with all those flash-bulbs from the camera going off in front of your face. No wonder you pose every time someone brings out a camera.

Then, the Sunday dinners at home were special. You, your dad, and I would sit around the table after dinner to talk of daily things. Relatives came by to visit and Sunday was the only day we could call "our own" day. Vegetables and Fisher Price helped you to grow.

My first born, I apologize for all the things I did not know. But look at you now; you are a responsible young adult who hardly ever drinks soda and who puts broccoli in spaghetti. You were born and raised during a time on an early morn. My apology if you were pushed ahead at an early age. My congratulations to you for demanding what you do from yourself. Let us shake to what first born make.

The Library

It was a home away from home. The Woodland Public Library welcomed all in the cold winter rain, on a cool spring evening, and in summer's blistering heat.

It was the home of giants: John Steinbeck, Samuel Clemens, Emily Dickinson, *Better Homes and Gardens,* and Apache Indians.

Any information or a lingering reading could be found within the shelves and quiet isles. Over a twenty year period, I came to watch it grow with computers and inter-library loans. I watched Brandon and Jane, the reference librarians, retire. These dedicated librarians helped me with research term papers, books on everything from writing well, water colors, abnormal psychology, to what Thoreau had for breakfast.

They directed me to why Samuel Clemens always wore white, why geraniums need a west or south exposure, painting being the number one home improvement, the City of Gold, and good parenting books.

My household grew, I grew, the kids grew. We became better individuals with expanded interests.

The library gave us a world to explore with weeks, hours, and years of growing into broader individuals. We had no time for boredom; we had new stacks of books every couple of weeks. We had new interests, new places to go, new goals, new conversations, and brand new days of wading through the world of books.

To this day, my grown kids recall our trips and our treasures which implanted activities that made a difference in all of our lives. Who would think that the Woodland Public Library, in its quaint little size, could bring such good things to a little family, in a little town, in such a big way?

Fair Play

There is nothing like a homespun county fair to remind us what is in our own backyard. It is a time of nice little surprises, and is full of our history, community, and resources, not to mention free things. It speaks of the generations before us, the present, and those to come. People come from all around to join in the biggest fashion show of the year, the latest gadgets, fair food, and to see old friends not seen in years.

Over the years, the fair has brought lots of memories in many forms. Thirty-eight years ago, I was so excited to attend. I took Ernie, our first born, to the fair when he was only a week old, only to take him back home knowing he was too young to be there. One year I was confined to a wheelchair due to a cracked foot, and attended with pleasure. I have lost one of my own kids in the crowd of hundreds of people and found him in the security office. I have also found kids and turned them in. We have stood in line, in a hundred degree temperature, so that four little kids could ride on make-believe animals and cars. We have won fish in pink water, drinking glasses, skates, stuffed animals, and walkie-talkies. In the seventies we booked a dinner for six people using water-less cookware, and received a vegetable slicer as a complimentary gift that we used for forty years.

The Yolo County Fair is a spectacular show. It is full of diverse people, animals, food, crops, talent, art, culture, fashion, everyday life, a slice of New York, and a hunk of the farm. It reminds me of a Mardi Gras in full swing. Put it all together and it is sprinkled with a bit of marvelous magic. One can almost see the glitter in the air and we certainly hear it. People drop what they are doing to attend. They even get out of their cars differently as they shut car doors faster and harder in their haste. It's a hurried sound as if one may miss something if one does not hurry. Some of the sights will not be seen again until next year and some sights will never be seen again. Different styles, anywhere from Kmart to Beverly Hill's Rodeo Drive can be seen. There is glamour as people don their statements in dress-up or come as you are. One can see high cuts, shorts, boots, flip flops, heels, gold chains, pearls, Hawaiian prints, and plaids. You can see sights of anything from a ninety-year-old woman with dentures eating a candy apple, to a toddler falling asleep while eating an ice cream cone. Singles go, newlyweds go, and entire families go. It is a time to join together, to have fun, stand around, walk around, meet old friends, and hug people. It is a time of celebration.

The air is full of nice smells that we don't smell every day. The Netherlands' funnel cakes, China's egg rolls. Mexico's tacos, the U.S. barbeques, handmade candy and popcorn fill the air and flavor the mood. It's like going out of town but being home at the same time, a tribute to one and all.

The midway people are respectful of the visitors and are part of the magic. Some are traveling show gypsies and part of the show, and some are everyday families. It is a life on the road we will never know; only touch on once a year. Their hard work, and many local individuals, bring all of us to a festive time; tie us to the richness of our community, to each other, and a little county fair. We are homespun.

A Tribute

You know what I loved about the fifties and sixties? It was a time of pure innocence; a time before anyone was guilty of anything big. Even though parents said "be careful," once out of sight, the world was ours. We ventured to half-filled canals to catch polliwogs, swung on flagpole chains, put saved nickels in jukeboxes at a corner hamburger drive-in where hamburgers sold six for a dollar. Quite a few times, we listened to Elvis while watching the older kids, sitting close in '57 Chevys. We didn't care what we looked like at that age, our hair a mess from flying on flagpoles, our pollywogs swimming in little buckets, and going steady made us giggle. We must have been a sight to see. The braver gender traded frogs for marbles or lizards and snuck into movie theaters, and felt so cunning all the way through the first half of the first feature. Choices, good or bad, were a time of learning. At least that's what our parents said.

My first pair of shoes I bought myself was a poor choice. They were candy-apple paten leathers that were shiny and beautiful. It was love at first sight. Once I had them, I realized they were just a little too fancy, and even though I only wore them a few times, they just fell apart and I went back to my oxfords. The big, bulky black and whites that cost five ninety-nine a pair and lasted until I out grew them. I looked like a chicken and walked like a duck because my feet were bigger than my legs.

Little did I know, when I started Woodland High School in 1965, the paten leather shoes would be outlawed because our mother dean insisted on protecting the virtue of every female, and declared the boys could look into our shoes and see up our skirts. Her most famous, and favorite, saying was "Why buy the cow if the milk is free." She walked the campus halls with a ruler to measure our skirts or dresses to make certain they were long enough. God bless the memory of Queen Carol. She had the best intentions. My dad's favorite saying was "When you make your bed, you have to lie in it." Good grace, no wonder at times we were a bit scared. Our parents had the same intentions, but a fib from us brought an inch of freedom.

One night in the middle of winter we girls told our parents we were going to the movies. Instead, a hot dog roast was planned on the outskirts of town at Steven's Bridge, even if it rained. It did rain and we had wet hot dogs. We didn't mind at all. Sitting on the large rocks, in the middle of nowhere, in the middle of the night, watching the smoke rise higher and higher and the soft rain falling on us, made it seem like we had never had a hot dog before. And we hadn't. Not like those in the middle of our fib and in the middle of nowhere. The night was so delightful, it was almost shameful. Then we girls climbed back into our '52 Studebaker, turned on the radio, and listened to the top ten as we drove back into town, wondering what the movie was all about.

Stepping back into the fifties, Mom and Dad bought a new house and a new car. Mom was so happy with the house, she said she could wax the floors and they'd be her floors and not someone else's. We didn't keep the car. They said it wasn't us. I think they meant the same thing I later discovered about my candy-apple shoes. But neighbors said we had the prettiest house on Cherry Lynn Drive. We had backyard carnivals, homemade theaters with stages, and talent shows. Our parents loved picket fences, tree forts, the president, and the Sunday morning newspaper.

Coming back to Woodland in the sixties, Keds tennis shoes came as fast as the bloomers came back in. For four ninety-nine a pair, one could own a rainbow and a pair for every day of the week. They were as common as Aqua Net Hairspray, black eyeliner, the Beatles, Beach Boys, Rolling Stones, Janis Joplin, the Supremes, kids running out of gas, and parents shaking their heads back and forth saying, "Would you look at that."

Well, it all passed. Woodstock was a statement to the end of an era.

The new era was announced by going to the moon. I miss it all. Gone are the guys wearing Town Craft t-shirts from JCPenney's because the shirts looked so casual with Levi Straus. Gone, old fashioned deans, home ec. teachers with buns pinned on top of their heads, and gone the buffalo nickel. The era ended quietly. But not really, the baby boomers are still here and the fifties and sixties still hint to be with memories, firsthand knowledge, and stories. The boomers were a part of it all. Just look at our kids, the remnants of a simple time that lingers in the halls of a history that rubbed off on all of us.

First Love

In *A Midsummer Night's Dream,* William Shakespeare said,

"The course of true love never did run smooth."

Alfred Tennyson said,

"'Tis better to have loved and lost
Than never to have loved at all."

Abraham Cowley wrote in his poem, "Gold,"

"A mighty pain to love it is
And 'tis a pain that pain to miss
But of all the Pains
The greatest pain
It is to love, but love in vain"

In the beginning I was in denial, and later love made me flee to higher ground. He was not in love. I ran and did not look back. This experience, to that extreme, happened only once in my life. My personhood's safe, quiet silence and oneness with myself, was shaken. After a period of denial, love felt nice like a spring rain in the middle of summer. I felt tickled, a rich joy, and I smiled a comfortable smile inside. However, he only had a small spark of interest. His interest was nothing more than an awareness of another human being due to respect and consideration. He was not turned inside out, upside down, head over heels, nor bumping into himself. I traveled that road alone. Instead, he was cool with senses intact and detached, which only made my road bumpier.

I had double jeopardy. I was darned if I did and darned if I didn't forge ahead; so I sort of shuffled my passage during those days. I was on a one-way street, with red rose petals and bright stars in front of me, and skid marks behind me. There were no stop signs, no yield signs, only a one-way arrow. Cupid, stupid Cupid, only to shoot one arrow. I was certain that everyone knew and I would be a part of mass media. I kept waiting for it to be announced on the five o'clock news.

As time passed, I lingered in the vicinity of the crime when the element of shock wore off. I waited for something small: a glimpse, a scent, a hello from across the room. I would have settled for anything. I went to the doctor for a remedy, just like an old song says. I took vitamins, changed the color of my hair, ate less, ate more. I worked more and then tried working less; I pampered myself. I even went out of my way to make new friends and I broke with those who harshly judged me. I tried to escape the clutches of love. But it was etched in time.

Love, I finally accepted it and went away a bigger person. It was no accident; it was part of my life and a chapter of myself. It was what it was, and a decade later what was carved into the pages of my days, my heart wrote:

Way back then
I bought new dresses
so he would see me
my spirit young
Heart full of Shakespeare
even heavy rain dropped sweet scent
he did notice
and left sonnets
old footprints
as he passed
as he walked beyond
Now decades later
I sip an extra cup of coffee

as I read the sonnets
smell the soft rain
and wear old dresses

First love—first love made me grow and love others and myself even more.

Little Notes

Lillian Hellman says, ". . . at any given moment you're only the sum of your life up to then. There are no big moments you can reach unless you've a pile of smaller moments to stand on . . ."

Those moments were how life functioned day to day and hour to hour in the changing days of time. Running one's life, one's household, or belonging to a family is a full time business, with the much needed and welcomed help of everyone. Everyone gave some, some gave more. Here are little notes of our efforts. Little notes of our lives.

San Diego trip—*Ernie, feed fish and Paulie two times a day. Let Paulie out in the yard, open door and air house out, water lawn and flower beds; Monday morning put dumpster on the street, please vacuum. Do not use the black light, may cause a fire—no alcohol—do not leave clothes in dryer and leave; change fish bowl every three days. I'll bring you something. If I am not back by Monday, pay $50.00 to the phone bill at Corner Drug; the bill is in the basket on the counter—Thanks. See ya soon—love, Mom.*

Sara and Chris, you can have the steak and beans—Chris, "share," I'm at the fair—love, Mom.

Mom, I came by and no one was here so I went home—page me when you get home, Josh.

Sara, could you keep an eye on my clothes? Just turn the knob to permanent press—spin cycle, Ernie.

Chris, leave my car here; I have places to go—it's 5:10 and I went to the bank, Mom.

Mom, I went to my dad's house, Sara.

Mom, Aunt Wilma called—she wants us to go to church with her tomorrow; they are having a pot luck. She wants you to call her—love, Sara.

Brenda, had a good open house—thanks for the soda, Phil.

Mom, went to Jeanine's house. If anyone calls me, take a message and then call me, Sara.

I go to bed tonight and think of the years the kids' father and I have put in with the kids. They are teenagers now with Ernie and Chris entering into young adulthood. Ernie lives with roommates, Joshua lives with his dad across town, and Sara and Chris live with me. We refuse to be torn apart by the divorce. We are in and out of each other's households. George comes to visit and I sometimes stock his refrigerator. We are friends now, and Daniels Street was yesterday's decade. It is planted as part of all of us and helps to enrich our days and days to come. Time marches on. We do the very best we can do, and I see that is well enough. As well as most, and better than some.

Chris, feed Paulie and tie her up on the back patio if you leave. If she barks, let her in. Go see Sara tomorrow if a friend can take you. Have Mike and Mandy go with you. See you when I get back from Idaho—I'll call you—love, Mom.

Mom, I called the California Highway Patrol—the freeway is closed right now due to an accident. The lady said we won't have any problems getting to the airport tomorrow—I'm at work now—love, Sara.

Mom, I went fishing with Javier, I'll be back to fix my car—love, Ernie.

Mom, Ernie called at 10:15—call him, Sara.

Mom, I left for work at Rico's—if Paulie isn't with you, please call me—love, Sara.

Mom, went to Lisa's—light the pumpkin, Sara.

When the kids were younger, we would make banana-nut bread and sit by the fire on Halloween night. We'd tell ghost stories or spooky true stories that always had some exaggerated details. Now that they are older, they dress up in gaudy costumes and join their friends at someone's house. Sometimes, I wait up in case they want banana-nut bread and to check the time they come in.

Mom, I came by and you weren't home; I'll stop by later, Josh.

Mom, went over to Dad's house to watch television. It's 7:30 p.m.—love, Sara.

Chris, please mow and water the lawn and front area, and rinse the patio off—Charlie's mom may come for dinner, Mom.

Mom, Phil Miller called. Chris.

Mom, I turned in a couple applications today and things sound pretty good. Sandy had just left when I got to B.P. They gave me a new appointment, and I saw Emily and she gave me a ride. I get to visit every Saturday now. Chris.

Mom, I came by and cleaned the yard as best I could because it was dark. I'll be home tomorrow afternoon to clean the rest and to play with Paulie—it's 9:40, see ya tomorrow—love, Sara.

Mom, Trishe from work called and she wants you to come in at 1:00 instead of 2:00 and to call and confirm it. Chris.

Mom, had Sara take me home—I was tired and I'll be over tomor-row, Ernie said he'll be over tomorrow—love, Josh—P.S. congratulations on graduation.

When I went to college, the whole family went. I owe so much to the kids and to their father while getting my degree. I worked, had the kids, ran the house, and went to school part time. I attended school from 1983 to 1995, sometimes only taking one or two classes at a time; finally getting my Bachelor of Arts from Sacramento State. The kids and some of their friends were in the audience cheering and whistling as I reached for my diploma. I owed it all to them and threw them a big kiss. They were the best. As their dad said "hold down the fort." They were raised with my humor and tough love and their dad's easy going nature. We all graduated; it was for all of us.

Mom, go look at the front yard. I mowed, trimmed flowers, and pulled some weeds in front. Chris.

Mom, I put dishes away and loaded the dishwasher. Love, Sara—P.S. thanks for our presents.

Hey Ma, we came by today about 12:30 and you weren't here. We made fresh tea, sliced a little ham. I did some laundry and hung it up. I pulled some weeds and dead flowers in the flower bed. We would have done more, but you weren't home, and we didn't know what you wanted done. We also did dishes for you. Love, your favorite daughter, Sara. And Missy says hi—we love you.

Brenda, this is all I could afford this week; at least it will cover the child support, and I'll make the rest up on the 21ˢᵗ. George.

Brenda, I polished my nails while I was sitting here. After I washed your dishes for you, Ernie and I had a nice visit. Your little home is precious, and I was wishing for a moment that I lived here. Your bowl that I washed, the clay one, you shouldn't use it; it is cracked and it can collect bacteria in the crack and make you sick. So don't use it for food anymore. Love, Sis Shirley.

I woke this morning thankful for my family. I stepped out on the front porch in early morning with a cup of coffee to start another day "in the life and times." I smiled, dressed, and let the kids sleep in as I became head of my household again. The kids' dad said I did, and do, a good job.

Sara, would you throw my colors in the wash before you leave? Thanks, Ernie.

Mom, Josh and I came by at 10:00. Can you give me a ride to work on Monday? Chris.

If Ernie calls, tell him I need to take his car to school tomorrow so my shop teacher can look at it. Just drop it off in the morning at my house. I will need to take it on Thursday to work on it. Josh.

Mom, I ran to Yuba to register. It will only take a few minutes—it's 11:20. Sara.

Mom, I stopped by to say hi, but you weren't home, Love, Josh.

Mom, I'm sorry I didn't have time to wash my skillet. I had to leave for work in a hurry. Chris.

Thanks Mom for doing my laundry, you're the best. Off to Tahoe. Love, Ernie.

Mom. Ernie called and he forgot about his white clothes. I put them in the dryer and he was wondering if you could get them when you get in— thank you—it's 7:20 and I'm going with Jeanine. Love, Sara.

Kids, I'm visiting Aunt Wilma, come over. Love, Mom.

Mom, could you throw my shoes in the wash? Thanks, Ernie.

Lillian Hellman also says from "Autumn Garden": ". . . that big hour of decision, the turning point in your life, the someday you've counted on when you'd suddenly wipe out your past mistakes, do the work you'd never done, think the way you'd never thought, have what you'd never had—it just doesn't come suddenly. You've trained yourself for it while you waited . . ."

With a little effort now and then, we can bring so much help and joy into the lives of others. It all begins with each of us—a small piece of our time. For what we do and share today becomes tomorrow's memories. Little tokens, from those special occasions, but mostly from the regular everyday happenings of our daily lives are what really matters.

Our house and lives were busy. We all had work, school, errands, friends, and places to go. Sometimes, family life had been on the run. A few times, without planning, we've all showed up at the same restaurant or the same store—and many times—buying the same thing. We waved at stop signs or red lights. One thing we all did best was being there for one another.

What a glorious ceremony—the celebration of ourselves.

Remember Daniels Street

I am now fifty-nine years old and fifty-nine years new and my life is more than half over. It has been spent in the world of kids and now a new generation approaches: the kids' kids. But my world of kids will never be spent as it once was on Daniels Street in the 1980s.

It seems like just a few days ago, a few pages back, around the corner, four houses down, lights blazing, Ernie, Chris, Sara, and Joshua were in need of the mommy and daddy thing. They each really needed us when they became popular in our neighborhood for romping in the front yard at twelve midnight during a few slumber parties, doorbell ditching where no kids lived, and the adults did not like anything other than their own little doggies or friends who came for martinis and dinner. The kids also needed us when a BB gun accidentally broke out a neighbor's twelve-by-twelve front window. They needed us for prompts on cold school mornings when one of them was placed on the front porch, in the shivering cold, wearing a flannel gown, with the threat of sending her to school in jammies, or she could get dressed and fueled with hot oatmeal, sliced apples and cheese, warm cocoa, a hug, and the promise that Friday was on its way.

The big house on Daniels Street was home throughout the kids' childhood. It saw the life and times of not only Ernie, Chris, Sara, and Joshua, it saw kids who were invited and some kids who forgot to go home. How could I send kids home to empty houses where parents were at work and some parents worked twenty-four/seven, building castles in the air or paying for Christmas in the Caribbean. I, the stay-at-home mom, said, "It's okay: we have enough cookies." So, we often traded shelter and cookies for washing dishes and vacuuming. It also saw kids who stumbled through the front door, tripping over the threshold—friends of a friend.

According to the kids, descendants of royalty sat at our dinner table many nights. Uh-huh. Sometimes the visitors even put in requests for dinner's menu. Tacos were the number one request and one visitor named them Brenda Tacos because of my watchful eye that the recipe was not changed with one of the kids slipping in that artificial seasoning for a dollar nineteen. So it was Brenda Tacos every Friday night and royalty helped with dishes.

There were trips to the Bahamas, Europe, and Mexico, by other parents while I stayed back on Daniels Street to watch over the kids' friends who were usually there anyway. We hardly noticed the parents' trips; we were waiting on secret adoption papers to come through the mail. Just about when I tired of these foreigners, or when it was family time, that fell under the phrase "that's it," and we all went back to ourselves and to each other. We had aunts and uncles come and bond and to share our food, other than Friday's tacos, and to hear stories that always leaked out when Ernie and Chris rode their BMXs on the two-story roof, whose turn it was to sit next to Mom at the dinner table, who got the favorite fork, and that all the kids were playing *Friday the 13th* with the meat cleaver again. Not to mention that family secrets were rolled out one by one, and Joshua even reported we'd taken out a five-thousand-dollar loan and why. "How in the world did he know that?" his dad asked. We must have forgotten to send him out of the room. I'd have to hurry him off to pick up toys in his room because of the legacy he gave to his aunts and uncles and the version of a six-year-old had a tendency to make me kind of dizzy.

Midnight house checks to make certain kids were tucked in their beds and kids down the street did not return with some kind of master plan. Bed checks usually started around ten p.m. and Calgon *never ever* took me away. It was similar to a twenty-four-hour group home where the kids' dads were not the only ones doing shift work. It was a time when turkey dinners came with real live kids from Turkey; and from some neighborhoods across town, our Danish rolls and German sausage brought two other countries who loaned us their orphans for authentic flavor. A few times imported beer snuck through an upstairs window all by itself. I would certainly not become the mom where all went over my head as the carpet was pulled out from under my feet. I'd not be the mom that the police officer asked at the front door if he could speak to whoever was in charge. It was my ship to maintain and to direct the crew with no one going overboard to abandon ship, and that included neighborhood kids.

With the demand of the kids' father's job I was appointed King and Queen of the house. A few times my crown was knocked off, but I put it back on after finding it under a kid's bed. I had a little country to run and I would not be deported by kids who needed directions to Comet, dog food, and the laundry room. Through it all, I had a helper.

Everyone has one in the family and ours was Joshua, the little brother. I found out all of the comings and goings and any plans in the making. When I had to step away for errands, supplies, sanity checks, or having less than three eyes, Joshua was my Channel Three News. He was a great journalist and undercover agent, and how he could report. Even when his brothers cuffed him to the tree in the front yard for snitching, he still went back to what he was good at. He dusted himself off, like I did with my fallen crown, to defend his place in the family. His brothers were placed on home arrest by me. Between the two of us we could have represented the CIA, the daily newspaper, and written the horoscopes of all that crossed the threshold at 742.

With teenagers and little people, odd music, and hair cuts that I had never witnessed in my lifetime, I learned to maintain order by spring cleaning every two or three weeks with lots of chores done daily. But some kids around town could not be found at spring cleaning time. Some kids were drawn to us and stuck it out until the end. I counted heads, dished out rakes, vacuum cleaners, scrub brushes, cleaning supplies; and one year we extended the driveway and the front walkway. Pizza was the ticket that got the show going.

Hup, two, three, four, Hup, two, three, four: Schofield, Christen, Chadwick, Barton, Harrison, change the vacuum cleaner bag, clean out the pantry, change the kitty litter box, find a box for lost and found—all soiled towels downstairs, all shoes upstairs. Miss Sara, find my France in a bottle, Joshua, keep recording and reporting—no deserters allowed. The kids were busy during the construction and demolition and when all sparkled and glittered, they were a good kind of tired. I was the headmaster and key to freedom.

After the Christen kids recovered and recuperated, we usually had "family day," and went on an outing to the zoo, of all places. Also, we went to the pool, to Arden Mall in Sacramento, or to the Woodland Library. The Tommys down the street or across town sadly were not included. We hung a "Do Not Disturb" sign until we returned and had a family discussion session with the intention of private therapy. We all aired our feelings and knew what each had concerns about and also what was demanded of each in order to stay in the family on good terms.

The four kids sat with hands folded in laps and had the look of pure innocence, except I could recall last week and Miss Peabody, her new roses and a continuously flying football. I could recall the dummy tied with a rope and placed in the street lying face down, while kids hid in bushes and tugged on it for passing motorists to see.

I could recall an old dilapidated barn built in the 1800s, in a nearby field. The barn was off limits but they made it into a secret clubhouse after many warnings. Also, I could recall a few castaways thinking they could actually enter, live in an upstairs bedroom, and not be discovered.

With kids sitting in a cluster in the family room, we heard everything: *He hit me, why can't I go, why do I have more chores than the boys,* and *can Rick, Shannon, Ryan, or Billy live with us? You pick one, Mom.* We dusted one another off and were good for another few weeks.

A Christmas holiday brought shampooing rugs, paint, and an explanation that *no,* the president was not coming to our house, but we were going to prepare as if. Four kids stood around waiting for some miracle to come and save them. The kids called me a workaholic; I told them it's *Momaholic.* If any neighbor kids came to the door and we announced we were spring cleaning, some took off running for home. I could not lure them in with chocolate pie; they knew it came with cleaning supplies. Adoption for the day sometimes never worked with the ones whose parents gave them BMWs, Mercedes, swimming pools, or credit cards. But, often we had plenty of loyal kids, the regulars, and I could never prove they were dodging their own cleaning days at home. Half of them tried to sit in during our family therapy but got dismissed at the door for coming down the wrong birth canal.

Then there was Whitey, the schizophrenic with hair the color of his name, who lived next door and everyone loved. The kids said, "Mom, he needs us; he's home alone all day. He can't go to school because of his illness and medicine." So he joined us and didn't look or act much worse than the rest of the clan. On some school days he would come over and keep me company for a while and then return home, only to come running when he saw the kids home from school.

After ten years, it ended. I suppose it ended slowly, but it seemed like it ended all at once. The kids grew up and one by one they went to college or got jobs. Some in non-traditional ways, but they went. Ernie went into real estate, Chris went into sales for solar, Sara became a nurse, and Joshua works for the county and the fire department. Along with his camera, he still records everything.

The neighbor kids and kids across town all have jobs and families now. They still come around after all these years and often we see one another during holidays, barbecues, or somewhere in town. They all say the same thing, "Remember Daniels Street? When are we gonna have Brenda Tacos?" In fact, I just got a request in my e-mail the other day from Hawaii echoing that familiar plea.

The kids are all now in their thirties and forties. Thirty years have passed; and when the kids come around, including the old neighbors or kids who lived across town, I give them tacos, without the artificial seasoning which they now request. I also serve them pie or cake; and I hire them, one by one, to help in my garden, or to paint, or just do something. Some things I never seem to outgrow.

Happily, all is not lost. In addition, I have the grandkids and I help them with their own Daniels Street now. Once a queen, a CEO, or a mom, always one. Once upon a time . . . Well, you should have been there; it was our "Blue Heaven."

My Friend

A dynamic get-the-job-done kind of woman. Don't cry over spilt milk, just clean it up and go on. Gail is an intelligent, strong, and organized being. She is witty, warm, and fun to be around. I feel fortunate in saying she is my favorite friend of all the friends I have had in my lifetime.

Over the years, our interest in vacations, children, and life have been similar. We vacationed together, watched each other's children grow, and encouraged one another through good times and bad times. Our conversations have included everything from gardening to the Mafia. We have laughed and cried together. She tells me when I am right and when I am wrong. Many times, we have danced, exercised, colored our hair, and been through one another's divorces together. Once, we even thought we were related. Her birth place is Mississippi; my grandfather was born in Mississippi, and her mother looks like my sister.

On our camping trips, our energetic spirits have been matched. In the wilderness, we have cleaned our make-shift house in the dirt and sand as we kept each of our four kids clean by heating a pan of bath water on the fire in the evening. We have ridden inner tubes down winding rapids, hiked a mile in the mountains to collect berries and crab apples; and we have sat on large rocks shaving our legs beside the creek. We sang songs when neither one of us could sing, told and kept secrets and crossed our hearts not to tell. We have made chocolate cake, pizza, and fresh baked bread, with pine trees above us, in the middle of nowhere. Our favorite time has been early morning, putting on coffee while everyone was sleeping. We could smell the woods and the coffee around us and all that morning offered. We have washed our faces in the creek, brushed our teeth and hair using a mirror hung on the side of a tree, and then sat and enjoyed the quiet morning. We have shared all chores, and in the evening, at the close of day, we have sat around a campfire telling stories and things of long ago. Together, even in the wilderness, we have been law enforcement, attorneys, politicians, nurses, teachers, and referees.

In sharing our lives, she has helped me to be me. I have witnessed her strengths and her weaknesses, and she has witnessed mine. She has influenced me in many things; we are allies. I only hope she has received something special in return from me. I know I may never have another friend that I feel so attached to as I do with Gail. We have grown, aged together, and felt and known our youth.

Now, after forty years of friendship, we meet at Denny's or somewhere for a quiet lunch. We chat, we laugh, we reminisce, we tell our secrets. She sends me a card on every holiday, and I send her a postcard when I am out of town. How fortunate we are to have one another, and to have had our paths cross years ago. My cherished friend; my endless memories.

Christmas of '88

It's Christmas day, I feel compelled to put a few memories on paper to record them from a small piece of history in the days and times of kids growing up and what does and does not work. The kids have always brought strays home to live out their lives. It never mattered to them weather the strays were animals or real live people who were displaced for the moment. Many times I had to tell them that moment would pass. But this Christmas they outdid themselves.

First of all, they know that I would divorce their father for Elvis Presley. Joshua, the youngest, came into the kitchen in the middle of me Windexing the window and asked me the question of the month.

"Mom, come look in the garage and please, can we keep him? You'll just love him."

I knew right away that whatever was in the garage was alive and probably hungry. Even on Christmas the kids were out looking for new members to recruit to our clan. I opened the garage door and standing on my load of white sheets I was in the process of washing, dripping clumps of wet mud, was a 250 pound Golden Lab. This was the largest thing the kids ever brought home. He was a giant and I was in a state of bewilderment. I thought we may need a crane or a lift to get him out of the garage. The youngest said with hope on his face, "Can we keep him; he's a purebred?" Chris, then fifteen years old, came to Josh's aide and said, "He's yours, Mom. We named him Elvis." Sara stood with one hand on the dog smiling with high hopes.

"I'm sorry, kids; he belongs to someone," I proudly told them. "A dog that can eat ten pounds of dog food a day named Elvis will not tie my heart strings in a little fancy bow. I can get better effects from listening to Elvis' 'I Did It My Way.' Please remove him from the laundry; put him out on the sidewalk to wait for his owner. He has tags with a phone number. Someone call quickly and be careful moving him. Bye-bye Elvis, and Merry Christmas."

After a phone call to the owner, we discovered the dog belonged to Ernie's previous English teacher. Ernie, the eighteen-year-old, had been the mastermind who for a moment was master of ceremonies. The dog was picked up and the kids all had sagging smiles. But I told them, "Imagine that. For a while Elvis was in our garage." Christmas . . . and to all a good night.

Teacher of the Year

How does one measure a great teacher? Do A's and B's at the end of class stand for a job well done? Or is it something students take with them long after class is over? My particular event with an impressive teacher was his ability to move students with his desire and talent to teach. He promoted positive thinking, action, interest, academic growth, inspiration, and from those: personal growth. Personal growth may have been something as simple as looking at situations differently which produced positive views. Positive views brought better selves and broader understandings.

I often thought that every student should be blessed with James Lawson. My opinion was matched by many of his students who were endowed with his discourse of teaching. His lectures were eye openers for all of us. They encouraged one to salute life. He entered the classroom with all the qualifications and desire to bring out the best in his students. Years later, I wish to return and drink from the fountain once more. When I recall his classes, I am left with an impression of a preparation, a foundation he gave to his students. I am inclined to say students were not only learning in his classes, they were entertained due to the wide variety of subjects and topics presented with his enthusiasm and vibrant interest. Our job as students was to take the material out, look at it, put forth the thought, the action, and address it as we developed a greater understanding of situations, every day issues, and problems around us. We went a mile and grew an inch. We put subjects and problems on paper, read them aloud, and saw things differently. We wrote and rewrote as we shared out lives.

For example, we gathered material for living as we walked daringly across swaying bridges, made mud cakes in the rain, and ran excitedly through strange streets as young kids. We were close to the ground and close to the sky. For fifty minutes in James Lawson's class, we simply were. We looked at our neighbors and really saw them. We read our living diaries and wrote our own journals. We came to know why a person would steal, lie, or sell themselves; we heard childbirth stories, learned how to do an oil change, and we visited far away villages. We walked down halls of nursing homes, ran in the snow, made grape jelly toast, and saw the Monarch fly in slow motion across the room. We collected ourselves in shallow ponds and deep rivers.

Consequently, by sharing our stories and views, we shared our own political selves, and from that, we gained a form of control and a good sense of understanding ourselves in contrast to others. Indeed, the philosophy Jim Lawson used in his teaching was *empowerment*. It was evident as he once stated, ". . . I mean that people in class will be able to do things that they want to do more effectively . . . of having control over parts of their lives."

Now wait a minute, we got all this in English classes? You bet we did. His classes were about life; his classes were about all of us. In fact, in reading and writing, we studied the human condition in order to bring it closer to us, to study it, to examine it, to learn from it. In our responses to the material, students made statements about what each topic meant and the importance of that material.

Throughout, one could hear Mr. Lawson say, "You learn when you write. Name it; give it a name. If it's a flower, what kind of flower is it? Don't be general; show, don't tell." And once we named it, we knew what it was. And we knew what we were in relation to it. He led us to the spot where he wanted us to go, then it was up to us to proceed. As I have once heard: "A teacher opens the door, it is up to the student to walk through it."

After leaving his classes, I had to write an essay on whether life or books were the most effective way to learn. I thought of his classes and was reminded that learning involved both life and books. His classes were a combination of both. Lectures and stories were brought into class by all of us from the dusty roads of living; books gave us legends of others before us. There were many different backgrounds, but we were very much the same.

In our papers, we learned to defend an argument, the process and analysis of dying, the comparison and contrast of stereotyping, the cause and effect of alcoholism, even the description of a building. We learned how to tell a story, the pros and cons of censorship, and public education versus private education. We responded to everything from *A Rose for Emily* to "Why a Surgeon Would Write," and the list goes on. Our assignments were given with the intention of problem solving. Mr. Lawson's students loved his classes as they furthered their own development.

In the very last class I took from this remarkable teacher, he handed out a list of objectives and he wrote, "The classes that we all remember with appreciation are not the ones that were the easiest grades . . . honesty compels me to say that I was grateful for the easy grades, but I also felt cheated . . ." Mr. Lawson's classes were busy and involving and everything but easy grades. They were not only hands-on living; they were helping hands.

How does one measure a great teacher, or any teacher for that matter? I would be inclined to say, by his or her students. The students of Mr. Lawson knew they had one of the best teachers and a wide, vast learning awareness. We not only took hard-earned grades, we took the biggest slice ever of education; we took growth. That growth we received because of the push onward, his encouraging words, subjects that required thinking, his energy and inspiration along with our own efforts. He opened the door and invited us in. How lucky to have had such a special teacher in our formative years, even during adulthood.

Thus, what tribute to give a teacher such as Mr. Lawson, other than to say, he made a difference in our education, a difference in our travels, and a difference in our lives. An excerpt from Nancy Caiken, "We may have just been spoiled by the best." Most positively, teacher of the year and one of a kind.

Heart to Heart

The police officer who met me on the front grounds of my brother's house with the inside lights blazing hard and the front door opened wide, said, "What is your name? What is your name? What is your relationship to Richie? What is your name? You look a lot like him. Can I see your identification? What is your name? I'm sorry, your brother is dead."

The night became darker. Dead, dead, dead. Forever and ever, dead. Somewhere in the night my brother had left us. Yellow, blue, and red lights flashed across my face. I turned my face to the dark sky and screamed as loud as I have ever screamed in my life. I screamed as the house lights burned brightly with the black blanket of night sobbing around me. Valentine's Day—a heart for a heart.

My friend Charlie held me up as I began to slump to the ground. I was clinging to him, holding onto his jacket. My brother and I would not speak that night. The chocolate-covered mints I bought for him would never be delivered.

Suicide never goes away. Only the person is removed, but the act lives on and on. It's been fourteen years and it's like it just happened yesterday, we weep.

My brother, at the age of forty, left this world by his own choice, or rather, from his point of view, no choice. The authorities said alcohol gave him the courage to do it. He blew his heart out. They've seen it time and time again. Women turn to pills and men turn to guns. We weep.

Personality, nice family, beautiful home, nice cars, money, and something amiss. A bit of bitterness, sympathy, empathy, sadness, pity, anger, and questions; forever unanswered questions are now part of our lives. It's like looking out a window and never seeing everything.

It happened on Valentine's Day and that day will never be the same for any of us. It's over, just like that. No room for change or growth; no new flowers to bloom for him in his garden; no new anything.

A few weeks before the anniversary of his death, I feel a little low—reflective and somber. Back and forth I reason, I search for some kind of answer or some kind of comfort, some kind of sign.

There is a hole in the center of our family now. Someone is missing. Someone who needed us more than we knew. I refuse to reel that night over in my mind, but it comes anyway on its own. Year after year. We weep.

God how we miss him; his dark brown hair, his scent, his laugh, his jokes, and his being. We even miss his truck that he kept waxed and meticulous as if it were an extension of himself.

He showed no signs to us, his siblings, of taking his life. Even his doctor was shocked over the news. Half the town was shocked. We hid behind our doors and dark sunglasses because of our pain.

He covered up his battle as all was picturesque. The house was sparkling, the palms were trimmed and watered, the pool glistened as always. But many issues of how he felt must have gone unaddressed.

A family who did financially well and who had a hunk of the rock and looked better than typical in their California lifestyle. Was it lost love, divorce, depression, mid-life crisis?

So, as the anniversary approaches, I realize how we all live on the edge or in the middle of things. I notice how the wind can blow dirt along Main Street, leaving papers and clutter in the gutters on a gray day and leaves one feeling lost. It even looks like the stars were rearranged. Did my brother mourn on gray days? Did he not know they would pass? Did he not know that he'd love again from his lost loves?

His only niece, Sara, later, took the mints we had bought him for Valentine's Day, out of the glove box of the car as we drove to Sacramento, with tears streaming down her face, opened them and in a bold defiant manner ate everyone of them. I did not stop her.

"Mom, how could Uncle Richie do this to us?" she said. Then she held her face in her hands and sobbed like a baby.

As time comes closer to the anniversary, I talk more. Richie should have talked more with us. He should have let us know how he was feeling. I just know we could have helped. I plant more flowers, I hug a family member, a friend. I embrace my feelings and I am gentle with myself. This anniversary date is a rocky road. I push the gray away and I give mints to people I love, or to a stranger. I stay in the house when the wind blows.

Also, I think how confusing and complicated things can be, I move away from the edge of the cliff.

I am okay for another year. I look at the stars and see that no one moved the big dipper. For a while, it only looked that way.

Dad

I sat in the second row on the church pew. All the windows had long, cream colored lace hanging loosely. The carpet was hard gray and woven of tight weave. The music drew me closer into the occasion. Closer than I really wanted to be. My father rested up front on center stage. A stranger would read and say some last and final words.

White mums framed what looked like a garden in someone's backyard, for the exception of the banner that read "Father." It was a cold, hollowed winter day; as it passed in front of me without interruption. He looked to be sleeping and his skin was soft pink, as if he were napping before dinner. Gone are the days. "Daddy, Daddy," I whispered to myself.

A large flag lay folded on a stand next to the silver metallic box that he slept in, a tribute from his World War II days on The Eisenhower. The windows draped with lace shadowed the outside world with a faint, filtered light that lay upon the coffin like a veil. It reminded me of things I would never know. The music stoked softly in a garden of some kind of promise.

The swollen earth cradled another: give and take. "Daddy, my daddy. His tool shed left untouched, without warning of his departure. Fingerprints left from another day's project. A hammer left where he had placed it.

I stood before him, a little girl in a woman's body. The years rolled by me slowly. The white satin surrounded him like a halo, and the glow from the electric candles on the wall looked like soft stars that lit the room. My eyes filled with tears that spilled onto my chest. A small voice said *accept it, accept it*. I bent my head and cried for the things I would never know. Amazing Grace encircled in a swirling breeze around me that rolled up the isles and lingered on the pew.

I stood before him in a humble, quiet manner. I stood in respect to the man who had loved me, fed me, and who had given me a warm home until I left the doorstep of my youth. Aloud, I read to my father, a last poem I wrote for him, to be placed beside him in his final state.

All the words you did depart/Upon my childhood/Upon my heart/ We watched you work/You watched us grow/God watered the Soil/to make it so/He said you/are the tree/Upon your branches/ will be leaves

I folded the poem, slid it between his arm and his side. I walked out of the parlor into winter's blazing sun. My eyes stung from bright light and tears. One last time, Amazing Grace was playing above my head, far into the sky, and settling in the trees and on the sidewalks. I thought of all the things I had forgotten to ask my father. I cried for that loss under the bright forgiving Idaho sky.

Miss Paulie

If a pet is a pet is a pet, Paulie was more than a pet; she was more than man's best friend, more than words could depict her. She was a member of the family and stood her ground in place and time. She was a master, in order, in the canine world; she was the ruler of herself, her own leadership. Even though she was obedient, she let us know if we were wrong in our direction or command to her.

Sometimes, if given a command, she would stand there looking at me, as if to say "I don't agree and I'm going to get that point across by standing here in opposition as I look strongly and positively at you." And that she did, very boldly. On those occasions, her feet planted soundly on the ground, her body language told me when she thought she was right. She stood in a mild mannered way of defiance. She would patiently wait for me to accept that with a friendly glisten in her eyes, and in her calm disposition, she would display her gentleness, yet, her contrariety as she told me "no." She made me question my own wishes, my own sufficiency, my ownership and who owned who.

Miss Paulie Ann, a jet-black German Sheppard with tan markings and elegant in her forty pounds of pride. She was a bit conceited, but beautiful in her mannerism. We bought her in Sacramento when she was a four-month-old, oversized, floppy puppy. She was Sara's graduation present from high school.

After a year or so, Paulie was left in my care when Sara moved to her first apartment, but not before she taught Paulie how to rumba. Paulie would put her front legs on the back of Sara's hips and they would dance all over the room to spicy Latin music. Sara spent many afternoons with Paulie as her dance partner and Sara did a good job training her. Then, Ernie would come to visit and roll around the floor with Paulie, and we wondered if Ernie came to visit us or the dog. He spent many afternoons with her, and Paulie loved those times and all the attention; she glowed and was full to the brim with love. She was still young, clumsy, and not yet of a higher order to her breed.

As the years passed, Miss Paulie was truly a jewel. I then knew why law enforcement used the German Sheppard. You practically do not have to train them; one just has to tell them what to do and they do it. Paulie was extremely intelligent, loyal, obedient, dependable, loveable, and fun. She loved the outdoors and was always first to test the deep waters.

She was a grand guard dog, and inside at night, she positioned herself in the very center of the living room. Often, I wondered why she did not sleep next to my bed, until I realized that the living room was in the center of the house. She was guarding the entire house. She would sit erect like a bold statue; her beauty and her breed was a kind of power she displayed. Night after night she positioned herself in the center of our lives. The living room was open and not as secluded as other rooms in the house, and she had a panoramic view of it all. She knew what she was doing and she knew more than we did. She was a merit to all of us as she guarded our world.

A police officer once told me that a dog can smell aggression, and Paulie showed that on a few occasions when duty called. I did not have to call her; she came out of nowhere and in an instant was doing her job. A Pit Bull in our neighborhood that was known to attack was chasing me in a vicious manner. I ran with fear on my wings as I thought my moments of escape were numbered. Within an instant, the Pit Bull was at my side. In a flash, like lightening, Paulie magically appeared and placed herself between me and the Pit Bull and nipped hard and fierce; the Pit Bull took off running for home. It was obvious that Paulie was in charge. I hate to think what would have happened if Paulie had not been there. Later, we made a police report and the Pit Bull was locked up for a while. There was a question if he could even return home.

Also, Paulie let us know by her continuous barking if there was something, or someone, that was in question concerning our safety. When she did not like something, the hair on her upper neck would stand up and she barked a warning. Red flags went up, and it was wise for us to heed her warnings. We listened and obeyed Paulie. She was our police dog.

Paulie loved going for rides in the car. When I asked her if she wanted to go for a ride, she always took off running for the car. In her excitement she did something between a bounce and a hop. I chuckled and Paulie howled as she leaped into the car. It was as if I had given her the world. Once in awhile, I would stop and get her a vanilla ice cream, place it in a small bowl, and she would lie on the back seat in the little black Mercedes, and lap it up. A beautiful sight that was—a black German dog in a black German car; it was picturesque.

One fall evening during a soft rain, Paulie and I were driving down the street as wet, yellow leaves fell and clung to the little black car. Paulie was sitting in the backseat, in her shiny black coat, in the spirit of herself. I told her I was going to write a poem about how this looked. It felt beautiful. And I then knew, while driving down the street in the misty rain, wet yellow leaves clinging to the car in all of its glimmer, in all of its nobility, and in all of Paulie's goodness, we were the poem.

Sometimes during our rides, Paulie fell asleep. I often woke her and told her our rides were a celebration and she should sit up and enjoy the moment. Immediately, she rose, sat up straight in all her glory, and looked out the window. She knew exactly what I had said because I always talked to her as if she was a person and she came to understand most everything.

She loved all and all loved her. Kids played with her, babies learning to walk stumbled and fell on her, and little kittens pawed at her. Paulie's peaceful nature was at home wherever she was. For instance, I had two pigeons, raised from birth, and they lived in the backyard with their cage door open so they could come and go. They walked in trust beside her and were forever riding on her back. She was as gentle as a quiet morning and she was content to have them on the property.

Paulie and I went to live in Illinois for two years where it snowed in winter. I threw snowballs to her and she would grab them in mid-air with her razor sharp teeth. The snowballs would disintegrate and she would be so surprised in her search for them. Her face showed a pleasant look of innocent wonder and bewilderment as the snowballs disappeared in the air when she bit at them. When the snow started to melt, she would find a large area that had not melted, and there I would find her in quiet splendor lying in the very middle of the snow patch. What a sight that was with her black coat up against a pure white background. The two beauties demanded a remarkable note ability; it was paramount. It looked like a postcard in the making and I was so fortunate to be around such beauty.

Our neighbors had five acres that led to the woods behind our house. There were very few fences in the area, so I put Paulie on a dog run when she was outside in the yard. She could go all over the backyard while connected to the cable. Ever so often, she would break the cable and gallop across the five acres and disappear into the woods. While running across the acres, she looked like a wild stallion in full run, cutting through the air, running for freedom. I would let her go, knowing she needed a bit of room to run off her energy. Then, many times, once in the woods, her leash would become entangled in the fallen trees and brush; she always barked for me to follow her sound and come to her aid. When freedom called her and she needed me, I searched the woods in the rain or snow, even a few times at night with a flashlight, but I told her she had it all wrong and she was suppose to rescue me. Out of loyalty and appreciation, I let her enjoy the freedom when the wild called her name.

Her nickname was Girlie. I knew she liked that because every time I called her Girlie, she would prance, as if in a dog show, on her two front legs. She acted like the name was something special. She was eminent.

If there were such a thing as a soul pet, then Paulie was my match. Our souls were in-sync with one another. She was there by my side in an instant if I cried, and she would bark a friendly bark when I showed excitement over happiness. For fourteen years she knew about me and I came to know a lot about her. I loved to put my arms around her, bury my face in her, and hug her tightly. She loved that. I was so grateful to have had the honor, the loyalty, and her friendship. For me, no other pet could match her. She was once in a lifetime.

Miss Paulie died one summer day when I was out on errands. She was lying on the cool garage floor as if asleep. I am so sorry I was not home for her passage. After the fourteen years she had given to me, I would have liked to have been there for her. But things sometimes happen for a reason and perhaps I was not supposed to be there. Perhaps, in my love for her, it would have been harder for me. Instead, I am left with only the fond memories. The final picture.

I have saved Paulie's collar and leash as a keepsake. I see her once in awhile with proud owners walking her down the sidewalk and I know exactly what they have. They also know. I have stopped and petted her many times, and the owners tell me of things I already know. But, I let them go on out of kinship, out of memory, and out of tribute. My little, big friend; Miss Paulie Ann Christen.

Evening Comes Early

We are born in the East and die in the West. Evening is coming early. George is in the hospital fighting for his life. The tubes are a sign of the seriousness of it all. We pray for more time here on earth; here with us. The kids do not have an end right now. They are full of faith and Dad.

Over the years George has been a good father. He may not have said much at times, but he was always there when needed. He would always wait for his kids.

When the kids were young children, he always gave to them the things they needed or the things they wanted. He gave from his heart; and the long hours and years of hard work was for them. If they ever needed to talk, he was there for that too.

Also, he was there for the kids' friends. If any of the friends needed a place from the grasp of the world, George opened his doors to welcome them in. They could stay and George gave them a warm bed, warm food, and treated them like family; with no questions asked. All of the kids' friends loved George and said he was like a second father to them. He was their friend.

At birthdays he may not have picked out the card, but he made certain there was a gift that was wished for. Christmas was always full of cheer, gratitude and surprises. He always came through for his kids.

Often, while the kids were busy with their friends, George would wait for them to return; he waited for them. Now, they are waiting for him.

His kids have been given a little longer. Maybe, just maybe, they are being given a chance for a little more time with their father. A door is left open for a while longer. Each day, each week, they have a chance for one more memory, and one more visit with an old friend. For them, all too soon evening is coming early.

Peace and Comfort

"What forces made George find joy and fulfillment from dedicating himself to a family of six in health, safety, and comfort. There is no greater example he set to base much of your own lives on to follow. No one will ever think higher of you than you deserve than your parents. Honor their lives and memories; they are fascinating and wonderful people. God bless you."

—Rick Garman

"Brenda, Ernie, Chris, Sara, and Josh—We have all known each other for many years. And it was a loss to all of us when George went home with the Lord. It was a great privilege to have known the man. I had many talks, and a few beers, with him over the years. I am going to miss him and I know all of you will also. George was a cool and great man. I love you guys! Your friend forever and ever."

—Mike Haynie

We had forty years of friendship and were married twenty of those years. Thank you for the many years of visits, the goals, the holidays, and the day-to-day living. Mostly, thank you for our four children: Ernie, Chris, Sara, and Josh. They are wonderful individuals: what fine children and adults they have become. All those tiger talks paid off.

In your honor, it is my intention to visit our honeymoon spot at the Rustling Pines in Tahoe, and eat pizza by the lake. I plan to take a trip to Frisco and have spaghetti and meatballs, and come home early as we did in 1969.

Forty years ago, how quickly time has passed. With the kids, it is my plan to carry on where you left off. Your passing is mourned. It is in the mourning and contemplation, as we deal with our loss and pain, that we come out on the other side better and stronger individuals. I think.

Thank you for the big house on Daniels Street and insisting we buy it so the kids would have plenty of room for themselves and for their friends. I see kids all over town who now say to me, "Remember Daniels Street?" The now-grown kids stop me and tell me stories that I have almost forgotten. They have good memories of those years and you helped to create those memories. The memories live on. Those years were filled with everything from the tooth fairy, new bikes, proms, and kids learning how to do laundry and cooking. In addition, we will never go camping again without thinking fondly of you.

Dad, Mom, I'm home. Anyone home? What's for dinner? And, *can I go?* still ring in the air like an old song.

Even the exchange students, who were hosted somewhere across town, found their way to our house and left all of us with lively stories. What joy and celebration in sharing our days.

What comforting years as birch trees and green velvet grass framed our little plot in the middle of the block, in the middle of our lives, and in the core of our years. Little did we know, the influences, the people, the passing of time, would monument our memory for years to come.

Thank you, George, for celebrating all of us, and thank you for your years of dedication and commitment. Also, what a good job you and the kids did picking out the Christmas tree year after year, painting, helping me shampoo carpets before the tree went up, and all the spring cleaning in the middle of December.

Thinking back over the forty years, my first gift from you was a bottle of Arpege' from Corner Drug Store. Arpege', I shall wear it even when it is not a special occasion. I will remember apple fritters with coffee on Saturday mornings, the Sacramento Union, Andy Capp, the roadrunner, and the crossword puzzle.

This Saturday we will celebrate your life in our own backyard. We will be here at home and you will be with us. The grass will be like velvet, the November flowers will be in full bloom, and the trees will shade us. Friends and family will filter in and out of the house as we play home videos of all of us over the years. Friends will see you one last time. They all have their stories as they hold a big part of you.

My sisters said you made a fine brother-in-law. My mother and father said you were such a great son-in-law, they considered you a son, and the kids said you were the best dad ever. You were a good husband and friend. For forty years you left us your life. Then, with little notice, evening came early. We miss you George.

Your friend Brenda

To Wear Many Hats

Throughout our lives we wear many different hats. Except with women, and the different major roles they play, a great problem may arise if each hat is left on for too long. For within the long hour of wearing one hat to another, the woman may lose the one hat that makes her a better person. It is the important hat that enables her to wear all hats in a more productive way. It is the hat of herself and the core of her happiness.

Ann Morrow Lindberg writes in her book, *Gift From the Sea*, "What circus act we women perform every day of our lives." And in the performance, in the rush of our daily lives, often we women put ourselves on hold as we tell ourselves we can do certain things we want to do *tomorrow*. We tell ourselves one day we are going to do that. All too often the day never comes, and if it does, we don't except it because the time for ourselves is so unfamiliar. We have put others first much too long.

To illustrate my own problem with wearing all the different hats; I came to love each one, and I went from one hat to the other simultaneously and willingly, constantly. Within the distance of one hat to another is where the danger lies. My own hat, the hat of myself, was usually of such a short duration, as I reached for another hat and as demand and time required me to do so.

Throughout my days I wore the hat of wife, mother, daughter, sister, aunt, friend, and someone that someone knew. Within the hats I was a nurse, a doctor, a gardener, a handyman, a painter, a chef, a counselor, a taxi, a teacher, Bank of America, the girl next door, the apple of someone's eye, and American pie. The more I worked at all the necessities of my hats and life, the less time I allowed for myself. In doing so, many around me came to expect many things from me.

Consequently, in my free time I did encounter, the silence or slice of solitude was frightening. The hat of myself I did not know and became lost in the crowd. It was similar to fishing for sun fish for others as my blue marlin swam away. And that was fine with me. I loved my roles. Yet, time and demand came knocking at my door. The clock kept changing and I knew I had to change with it. Ann Morrow Lindberg writes, "One must lose one's life to find it." She states:

"How to remain whole in the midst of the distraction of life;
How to remain balanced, no matter what centrifugal forces
tend to pull one off center; how to remain strong . . .
We must relearn to be alone."

In the business of living I had to find my own private space; my own free time where I could be the person only, and to be my best friend with nothing else for the moment and no demands. For this purpose, I started saying no to everyone. I liked the sound of it and the results. I stopped going the extra mile. I then gave myself the gift of myself.

I stood under an oak tree in my back yard every morning at sunrise and listened to the quiet morning. I looked under rocks for things I had not seen. I placed a small twig in a dish of water and watched it float. I wrote a journal. I went alone and sometimes with friends out for lunch. I served frozen pies, went for country rides and read books. I said *not now* many times. I came into the awareness and importance I owed myself as an individual, as a woman. I then approached each hat in a fresher manner and with more pleasure. I wasn't as tired. I blossomed with color. Those around me benefited from my change and growth.

In conclusion I profess, if I am a tree, I must grow branches, if I am a flower, I must bloom, if I am myself, I must be who I am and not what others think they may want me to be. I must grow with experience and balance from that growth. The hats will be beautiful as they sing the song of myself first. The hats no longer will be my main purpose and will remain the best part of my life. However, my own hat I will wear the best. And in doing so, I will have my direction and my balance. I will sing my own song.

The Inconvenient Truth

Wallis Simpson says, "A woman's life can really be a succession of lives, each revolving around some emotionally compelling situation or challenge, and each marked off by some intense experience."

In 1983 I took a class in creative writing. Also, I was diagnosed as bipolar. It was a double jeopardy. Between the two, I didn't know which was worse. Sharing my stories with a bunch of strangers, feeling stripped to the bone, or feeling different and acting different because bi-polar came with wings and took off in flight. I wanted to run home where it was safe. But that would have made me feel like a failure. We had enough kids at home who didn't act their age.

It was hard to open one's life up, and sharing the writing, fiction or non-fiction, can be extremely revealing, giving others a glimpse into one's private life. Often, others may not separate the writing from the person and perhaps there is not a separation. I simply wanted to blend into the crowd. I thought if there was such a thing as normal, that's what I wanted to be in a unique kind of way. Instead, I felt awkward, different, and wide open.

Gail Sheeny says, "Creativity can be described as letting go of certainties." Believe me, as I was letting go, I was holding on for dear life. I suppose I was more of an introvert in a fast lane with no stop signs.

Ermma Bombeck said, "Women are never what they seem to be. There is the woman you see and the woman who is hidden." The writing class was double exposure. Everything seemed to be in conflict and in opposition to myself.

Little did I know, it was a time of growing and the challenge was the liberation of my own oneness in the relationship with myself. I did know that I did best with small steps, like walking carefully on stepping stones at my own pace. I assumed, at thirty-three, I had been through the major growing years. I could not have been more wrong. I had a lot to learn.

On the other hand, bi-polar was not new to me; it was merely named that year. I set out to prove my psychiatrist, which automatically comes with the diagnosis and the mental health people, wrong. I tried to run from a truth in my life. The truth hurt. However, one cannot run away from one's self. After a couple of useless attempts to prove the industry wrong, they won. I was sent away to rest for a week after taking some pills. Although I loved my family, I was so tired. School, my doctor said, was just another place that I had to perform and it was too much. I was on overload in overdrive. My doctor said bi-polar was not that hard to live with. It explained my cleaning at odd hours, nonstop for days. Lack of knowledge caused me to live with repeated episodes. Over and over I had manic days until I worked to exhaustion. I kept going to carry on my duties with family at my expense, not theirs.

Then, when the writing class ended I became melancholy. I missed the class and the time. I admired the teacher and all loved him. I had used the class as a form of therapy. With all the stories we had heard, it seemed like a movie we had all seen together. I would remember this growth. My heart was soft. I planned to take part B of the class when I was feeling and thinking better. I forged ahead to art and English classes at a slower pace. Something else was going on besides bi-polar as I felt turned upside-down and inside-out. I struggled to maintain an average composure, often going from bad to worse.

Now, in my second semester, my classes were so much work. It must have showed. My art teacher made attempts, perhaps, in a helpful way for me to return to the writing class. But I didn't want to burden any-one with how I was feeling. My bi-polar was in full bloom and I fought against it. The medication only took the edge off. I must have been a comical sight. And I asked myself, why me? I was in pain with no insight. I was innocent without being ignorant, not enlightened, with-out being in denial. I absolutely did not know the answer to this other thing that was going on with me. I was blinded.

One day while standing in art class, the teacher was speaking of the writing class as he often did. I listened and without any kind of warning it came to me softly. I was engulfed in a total darkness. Literally, I had no outward sight. I traveled somewhere unknown, in a place other than where I stood in art class. Whatever it was it lulled me, cradled me, and softly rocked me. I suppose I had to go there to retrieve my truth.

While in the soft darkness a gentle voice said, "You love him." Quietly, I was brought back into the light and into the art room. I was still standing and some were looking at me. I now had my answer to what the other thing was that was hitting my bi-polar in the center of itself. I had truth, my truth. No matter whether I like it or not, no matter anything. I felt a peaceful joy. I was the student who had fallen in love with the writing teacher. Crush? I told a friend don't even go there. It was no crush.

As time went on, I took my bi-polar with me and that silly girl thing as I tried to make light of my life. Leo Buscaglia would have said, "Hug him, love is a celebration." I went to Sacramento State University to finish my degree, and *the other thing* I took with me.

In honor, I raked leaves, as Buscaglia did, and brought them into my living room. The beauty of red, gold, and yellow leaves became a conversational piece at our house. They were from a tree of life. They were in their season, in addition to my own life. I embraced myself and wrote more to mend my heart.

A few people in our lives stand out above all others. Some not only help us through a transition, they are the transition. They were like stepping stones to greater truths which enable us to travel from one place to the next.

In tribute to it all, those years stood as a monumental time of growth. I learned to live with bi-polar and to love life a little more. I laugh more, sing more, and learn more. I'm kind to myself. I forgive others. I dance.

The Visit

California, the Knob Hill of art and free expression, sunny skies, beaches, San Francisco, sidewalk cafes, unfiltered opinions, and daring students who tested eccentric masters in "the land of the free and home of the brave." It's a place where culture and lawsuit come second to the credit card and New York.

Stepping beyond, only eighteen hundred miles away they'd heard all about us. Constantly, I defended the sanity of the entire state, our liberated life styles, our slipping into the ocean, our aristocratic approach to living the good life and our manic rush from one place to another.

I always heard comments like, "You folks are always fixin' up your houses, always buildin' somethin'. Ya got any room left for grass?"

There is an imaginary boundary, boxed and sealed, due to our own familiarity and our similarity within our own area. I, too, held tight to my own little corner of the world. I wanted to shake some of these people. Diversity is a friend not a foe. There should never be a divided line between what's better and what is right. I thought of owning a Ford Taurus instead of a Mercedes. I thought of a Big Mac versus a prime rib, a zirconium versus a diamond, and cotton versus velvet. One is not necessarily better than the other. It's a mental attitude on what's different, what's normal, and what's better. It goes from house to house, block to block, and yes, from state to state. I thought of the humor of it all, and what a state, the luxury of ourselves.

In Illinois, even though the death rate increased both in the winter and in the summer due to severe weather, just like Thoreau at Walden Pond, I welcomed what I might learn. I took a slower pace than I did in California. I walked through patches of wooded areas of young and old ash, oak, willow, birches, cottonwood, and box elders, and in awe of the dogwood, even in the middle of town. I enjoyed the cobblestone streets and visited shops that did not open at their posted time. Cornfields grew next to Quick Trip minimarts, unfenced ponds were fearless and charming; I was open to all things without judgment. In doing so, I welcomed the naturalness and the spirit of things in that part of the country. It brought to mind the work and determination of mankind. The arch across the Mississippi River was an example of how lives have stood in time for others.

However, some individuals did not like the California tags on my car. A few times people honked at me and screeched from open car windows, "Go back to California." Yet, many were friendly.

In all the differences, some wanted to come to California, to visit, and to see the state. For a while, they thought quickly and I thought slowly. Through traded stories and visual imagery friendships developed, and we became the other in a good way. The best came from both areas.

Before I left Illinois, I stood at the mouth of the Missouri River where Louis and Clark started their journey, their struggle to go where others had not. I thought of how Ben Franklin could have gone to Palm Springs and Abe Lincoln could have gone to Mexico. The boundaries we set should have no limits. My spirit branched.

I returned home to California where an Indian-village sight had been unearthed in our own back yards, where proud parents and students from a nontraditional high school graduated, with honors, in satin gowns. Our cities, we occupy by chance. Differences are all part of the whole.

An old Chinese proverb says it nicely, "Discover your companion's world. Two worlds are richer than one." After two years, I came home to California, but I still fondly recall slower, simple ways of charming summer days, brilliant white winters, and dogwood that grow wild in the woods.

Homesick

Home is such a small corner of the earth, a tiny speck. Yet I long to return to a place my heart lingers over the years with experiences and my little family. I long for familiar streets, a soft California rain, and those poppies that grow wild in a field that may get overlooked by some because of familiarity.

I dream of coffee at an outdoor café table, discount stores, and a favorite thrift shop on a Saturday afternoon. I dream of small talk and a newspaper with horoscopes that are fun, make me chuckle and remind me of the openness of one state that brings welcomed memories before I close my eyes each night. How I long to return and touch my memories.

My solitude with myself and the imprint of beaches, mountain streams, Tahoe's white winters, and a friend from high school, make me realize I have poppies tangled in my hair, sand between my toes, outdoor scent on my clothing, and my opinion expressed with the twenty-eight trees I planted in a twenty year period. The trees are with me, two thousand miles away. I want to see them and smell them. I want to go home.

My passion is in Woodland. It is simple, I am homesick. Memories flow and the letters I write keep coming with no end in sight. I spend part of my day gathering words to send and my heart writes the letters.

Looking over the years, I had great kids who allowed me to shine with them as they were growing up. The memories are endless. Once in the eighties, the kids and I leveled the backyard and hauled dirt out to the street. We must have hauled a hundred wheel barrows as we pushed on to beautify our little plot and to bond. We did the job of three men. It was not uncommon for me to garden at night with a flashlight, a cup of coffee, and home.

Coming home to help deliver my granddaughter, I had a cold drink at the airport in Phoenix with some artist. Here was a good chance for me to get tips on my own art, but I couldn't wait to get home and we talked of Woodland.

It didn't matter if Bellville and Swansea and parts of Illinois that I'd seen were quaint, lovely, and calendar material, with little bridges over lily ponds with cobblestone streets. The riverboat rides down the Mississippi, the dogwood blooming in the wooded areas, and the outdoor barbeques on almost every corner was not home. I could have been in Italy and I would have felt the same: homesick. You came, you saw, and you went home. I never once saw an orange poppy.

With respect, in all of the beauty of Illinois, I longed for where I had grown to adulthood and shared my life and days with big happening and simple things. California was in the center of who I had become. The biggest part of my life and how my life evolved is because of Woodland and home.

Jimmy D.

I try not to stereotype, but I divorced my second husband before I married him. Maybe I should have stereotyped. I prefer not to say he had an attitude, so I'll say he had a predisposition. However, I do have a few memorable moments; still shortly after the matrimonial passage I had a realization of the evolution of our union. Also, relatives were shaking their heads back and forth mumbling something.

Let me introduce you to my new husband. You've heard the story, the kids' new father. Well, not quite. It was never meant for him to take on that role, and the kids ended up wanting to exile him. I quote Mojo Nixon, "Have you ever heard of big rigs, UFOs, and barbecues?" Rockabilly, in the music world, that's Jimmy D.—a spinoff from James Dean, the Hollywood rebel. The kids thought a UFO had landed in our backyard and one of its occupants had come to scare us. They were partly right; he emerged from another planet. Somewhere out there.

Again I quote, "This man showed up in boots and ruined my black-tie affair, and he did have friends in low places." We just didn't go there.

He was an ex-race car driver, his legal way to speed and get away with it. He said there was no such thing as an ex. I wondered with my petitioned document from the courthouse, where did that leave me? I'd been with him on the freeway and viewed a polite, yet precise, demand for the car in front of us to move over. He was very proud of his heritage on the tracks and used his driver's license as a resume. It was like viewing a ballet. All the drivers assuredly moved over to let him dance. He knew how to line the wind up with the car in front of us that encouraged the other driver to want to move over. He used polite manners, dynamics, physics, and often the color of his car.

We were quite a contrast. He was a male raised in the fifties and I was a practicing feminist, because I was raised in the sixties. My letters to friends were signed anywhere from "See you soon" at a garage sale in Canada to "Having a ball in Modesto."

Jimmy D. and I agreed to disagree; yet, there was an element of shock that distracted me from time to time. I was reminded of him when The Beat Farmers said, "Find a dress, put your ass in it; we're goin' out for dinner."

After a year of marriage, my German Shepherd still barked at him. That is police dog to him. He loved rock, pork chops, Wienerschnitzel, and twenty-four-hour buffets. He was known to bring a piece of the world to me in the back of his pickup truck. That vehicle could be dangerous for him, and the presents didn't count.

Many times, he would twinkle in the eye, show his dimples and say, "Sweetheart, we're outa here." He got that right. I realized we could not go on. I had not only lived on the edge, I jumped off the blasted cliff.

I could just see his demeanor when he got the divorce papers. He probably had a serious look on his face, remembered the birch trees he brought me and said, "She's always tryin' to do somethin' fancy." No dimples showing. When my dad said I'd have to kiss a lot of frogs to find my prince, I'm sure he didn't have Jimmy D. in mind. To each his own.

We are now long-distance friends, and I just bought myself a birch tree. He said on the phone the other day that he was going for a pork chop sandwich and he asked did I want to come along. I said, "No, I'm going to water my birch tree and steam some squash." He said, "Well I'm headed for the freeway." No doubt, he will probably dance his way across the country and end up back on that UFO.

Sisters

Sisters, the four of us wear one another's coats. In this life we are known by one another. If you see one of us, you see all of us.

We've shared each other's clothes, food, cars, house, and money. We've treaded a path of joy, and at times, a path of sadness. What belongs to one of us belongs to all of us. We are each other's best friend. We are there for the other in good weather and in the wind. We've won, we've lost. We've been real and known to pretend.

We have even paid each other's bills, shared secrets and pies, combs and over-the-counter pills. We are known to make and to cut deals.

We've watched one another's friends come and go, sat in waiting rooms at hospitals and graduation rows. The four of us have helped to bury a treasured pet, shared childhood memories we could never forget. We have moved the other from block to block and across some states, put up fences only to add some gates. Each have been early and pleasantly late, even stolen the other's date.

We would not give up anything for all the years we've laughed so hard it hurt and when we've wiped away each other's tears. As children, we drew our dreams in the dirt. A comical bunch of women we are, we're together near and far.

Shirley, once the baby, has the get up and go with coffee and probably a cream filled cupcake. She's like Cinderella going to the ball, every day, but head of her household in her five-foot-three-inches. She mends the neighborhood cats and helps with other people's kids. If you like her shirt, she will give it to you. She grows tulips, collects old things, rearranges her furniture, plants mini gardens, and finds bargains.

Wilma, who likes to go by Sue, is the business woman, the politician, the pie maker, and the holiday feast. She is the woman on the block who can save neighborhood kids from the world's destruction, with or without CPS, probation, or the judge. She listens, and quietly comes to the aide with results while carrying an arm-full of miracles.

Cindy, the change of life baby when my mother remarried, is a worker. She does the jobs that no one else wants. She remodels our yards that frame our houses. She makes us look beautiful as if we have done it all alone all along. She pretends to be tough, but cries over a song and a girl in a torn dress. She loves her comfortable t-shirts and her own style. We can count on her as our holiday help and at our holiday table. However, at a formal affair, she'll stay back and water our property and tend our flowers. She says she's too simple to dress like Hollywood.

Then there is me, the oldest. But I have a lot to learn by watching the three of them. They call me Martha Stewart because I fluffed my red pillows, planted an English garden, painted a pistachio living room with a plum-colored trim, and planted white roses that my neighbors pick. I am a holiday; not a legal, business bone in my body. But I have soft pink geraniums, a jelly bean jar, tips on kids, and things in the refrigerator. I watch and listen for a new poem or story and a new way to make rice.

We are what we are. We are passing through this simple, yet complicated life, hoping to make a difference in lives around us. Each one of us contributing to the legacy and numbered days of one another. We are fortunate to be who we are, to be a part of the joy and happiness of sisterhood.

A Letter to Idaho

Dear Wilma, Shirley, Cindy, Glen, and Clinton,

What a marvelous time and visit I had. Those memories will stay with me for always. I had a lot of planning and rearranging things here at home before I left. It was all worth it. It seems I am busier than ever before—now that I am approaching my sixties. I'd like to say to all of you that I owe you my most recent happiness and also a nice gift. Now don't say no. You girls know how I am. I'll send it with a piece of my heart.

What a charming area you live in. I can still smell the alfalfa, cut grass, and country farms. It was wonderful going to the pool, the Green Belt, out for pizza, to the movies, the dollar store, garage sales, driving the little blue car, listening to the radio, going to Clinton's apartment and to downtown Boise. Even all those cats were darling. I don't really want to kill them. Ha-ha! I shall never forget Wilma's big farmhouse, the country porch, and the pink sunrise in early morning. I know why I would get up so early. I didn't want to miss a thing. It was all so lovely and a needed break for me.

Even though I slept a lot when I first arrived, I was probably over-loaded from planning my trip. You know, that's how I get, in the beginning, when I attempt an adventure. I wanted all to go well. One does not always sit around an airport, hundreds of miles from home, waiting on the right plane, the right gate, the right ticket, the right destination at the right time without a bit of stress. I should be used to it, but I think anticipation every time I go on an adventure puts me spinning. Even with medication. We can accomplish a lot with bi-polar, but it does have its down side.

Shirley, thank you for getting up early with me and having coffee; I get up at four even at home. I can't help myself from that. I love the hour.

Wilma, thank you for all your thoughtfulness and just being you, not to mention rolling out the red carpet.

And Cindy, thank you for spending the night with Shirley while I was visiting. Thanks for liking my Chicana. Your potato salad was a pleasant change from my own.

Clinton, thank you for opening up your home and being my nephew. You have done a great job decorating and it was very comfortable. I loved the pine trees out your back door.

Glen, thanks for your understanding with us sisters for running so much, and putting up with my odd hours in the mornings.

I want each of you to know that in the early hours while you were asleep, and I rose very early, I would have a cup of coffee and just sit and absorb all of your lives according to your beautiful homes and your comings and goings. I just loved it. I also loved when we just sat around and did nothing. What peace and comfort. The silence in the country, the white owl in the tree by my bedroom window, the big farmhouse kitchen was so quietly restful. It truly was a day in the country. The best part was I had two weeks of it.

Now that I am back home in California, with all my situations, busy life, and grown kids who are my best friends, I feel so very blessed. My little home and kids bring me life. I learn from all of my family. Each individual brings something all their own that they contribute to all of us. Thank you for being a wonderful family and a day in the country.

Always,
Love Brenda

My Little Friend

Dear Deborah,

A few words today about your brother who has decided we are not friends again since the last time I called you. He gets his way now and then as our friendship is off and on, but eventually on again. He calls me Punkinhead and I then know all is well.

We went to lunch today and went to the park. The grass was cool and I stretched out amongst the leaves; Rick and I visited. Today is the first day of fall, and what a glorious day with crisp in the air. We had a good time. As you know, Rick does not get out much, his own choice, as he is a true recluse and hermit. I do feel honored to be able to share some of his days. It is good for him and I can see that he benefits from the change. I have never known a hermit and most people never will. The hermit stays hidden behind the walls they have built. The majority of people have only read of them in books. They are quite resourceful and have only themselves.

I have seen him turn down so many chances for friendships and invitations, not even wanting to be there in the first place. Rick moves to the back of the crowd and sort of vanishes. Often, even I cannot find him, and I know him verily well.

His house is clean and in plain style. He has nothing extra and the house is very sparse. He does not have anything he does not need or put to good use, except a large, oversized green and white Oriental vase that holds some cattails we found while on a ride in the country this summer. And he has a red Oriental room divider that he reluctantly splurged on. He looked at it three times before he bought it. Other than those two items, Rick is extremely conservative. He has no clutter, no hassles, just the way he lives his life. A few times he has talked about the two of us getting married. Then, he takes it back and I know he is just listening to himself talk. He is no more serious than poppies growing on the moon. But he dreams outside of his little world once in awhile. Plus, we are only friends, and he may be my best friend.

Sometimes, our friendship is threatened and is in question due to him not accepting my ways. He thinks I have too much fluff in my life and hates to hear of my shopping trips or some item I want. He truly has chosen to walk alone. A few times, I catch up with him, only to be left by the roadside while he goes back to his solitude and oneness. I usually stand there alone, holding my own hand, and ask what happened. I know what happened. He is a recluse.

However, I enjoy what friendship we do have, and cannot help but notice his humanness, in spite of him being a true-grit loner. I will forever have room for his life and our small talks, our ice-cream trips around town, television shows, and dreaming once in awhile. I find him extremely interesting on his path he has decided to walk, as I get a glimpse into the rarity of that kind of person and life. I think the world of my little friend.

Always your brother's friend,
Brenda

What I Might Learn

Grown kids returning home can be both good and not so good. Lives get rearranged in the change with lots of alterations. Christmas came early at our house this year, it came twice. My second son, Chris, came to live with my daughter and me while waiting on his new place. My daughter, Sara, was living with me due to having open heart surgery a few years earlier and had not made her final move. We had three separate adult lives messed together in a kind of rough harmony.

Family usually tells it like it is, often sparing no words, and family members have the knack to tear down walls to construct ramps for inside information that enable each person to know the other. One sees all and all see one.

Chris happened to be self-appointed head of family. I happened to *be* head of household. So, since I also live in my household—hello, we both have a job that reflects onto others, and we take the necessary actions to do our jobs within our family circle. I do my job from necessity; Chris does his job out of glory. Now, with him occupying my house he took on what he called "the voice of the family," a plot to regroup and rearrange. In an instant, he grabbed the job at my house. It's hard for me to relinquish head of household since I have run my household for almost a lifetime. So we bumped into one another once in awhile. He started out gently.

"Mom, you know we love you. I know it's Christmas, but everyone knows you have collected things without taking other things out of the house. You need the eye of another. You've got clutter, Mom."

He stood *my* ground and acted as if he were selling a product.

"Too busy, too full, too cluttered, it's time for a change," he said.

"That needs to go, that needs to go, and that needs to go," as he pointed positively and directly at objects around the room. We had a few words that flew through the air like little rockets. How dare him, I thought. I'm doing him a favor by opening up my home to him . . . "Unbelievable," I told him.

"Chris, I'm down to two totes of Christmas decorations; I thinned everything out last Christmas. I had throwaways and donations."

"Well, I'm not talking about Christmas. You need to discard some other things. Your house would be nicer and you'd have more room and less work. Look at this stuff, there's no room to sit or walk."

The girls I go to lunch with would not be happy that my son was attempting a makeover in my house. I could never live that down with the Martha Stewart club. I would lose my ground as head of anything.

The first thing he suggested was that my lattice shelf in the kitchen window come down. Out of the house, removed for good he had said. The salt shaker that required about eight steps from the counter preparation area in order to use it, slowly, constantly moved. In its new spot I found it at my fingertips. The little green checkered cabinet in the laundry room that held my garden gloves, garden shoes, tool box, and cat food needed a new home due to him stubbing his toe each time he passed it. He did not hesitate to declare all and went from room to room suggesting changes.

Shoulders erect, he looked like a prize fighter in the middle of my little decorated chateau. This thirty-five-year-old bachelor insisted the pistachio green did not go with the plum trim. I saw it in *House Beautiful* and it was charming. He insisted my colored bottles and pictures of the kids growing up were space takers. The pictures, according to his advice, could be placed in photo albums, and the little bottles I had collected when I was out of state could go to the recycle bin. He smiled and went on as I defended my choices, my territory, my personality, and my job as head of household. The salt shaker could stay in its new home but that's it. The small antique radio cabinet that I had bought in Modesto, now used as a book cabinet, and the old grape box from Davis that held photo albums of family life and captured years could stay, according to him, if I repositioned them in the front room. I smiled and let him go on. He was so matter-of-fact and sure of his judgments; he waited for no comments from me. He said he had wanted to do this for a long time. He said the entire family agreed with him. He went on as he was not anywhere near the finish line.

According to Chris, even my dish soap was located in an unhandy spot. It was too close to the food preparation. One had to reach over the food to in order to pick it up for use. So now, since he became a member of the household, the dish soap had moved to the left of the sink each time I reached to the right. In addition to his wisdom and thought, my computer room held too many trinkets and little things. But he liked the Elvis and Marilyn Monroe pictures; their era was for all time. It was my era that needed the makeover, he said. He carried on like an art critic, and I found humor in his courage of not only doing a makeover, but a takeover. He was a curator of all time.

He was nowhere near stopping as he proceeded. Too many throw rugs; just too many everything, you go overboard, he had said. I explained to him that I used the rugs for color. He said color came in a can. He placed his pole lamp in the kitchen and it looked like something that could hold the Statue of Liberty. However, the light from the lamp brought out all the color in the room quite nicely. I moved it near the wall, just for now I told him. My painting of red geraniums brightened the entire kitchen and I actually liked it. But I had to insist and stop him as he was in full command and getting his way on many things.

In the front room, in a far corner, he placed a six-foot candelabra that looked like it belonged in a medieval castle. The light from the candles flickered onto the walls and the room glowed and cast a warm light. Well, maybe it can stay, I told him. I am not saying it's for sure, but maybe. After removing a wicker chair he placed a small wooden cabinet that had red, green, gold, and purple small drawers that resembled an old mailbox, or account box from a corner store or post office. The chair found a new home under the umbrella on the patio outside the back door. "I can live with that, but I'll not have you move my white wicker far from me. I love my chair, I'm French-country here. Now stop, that's enough," I told him.

He was not finished and I was expecting to see a bulldozer parked in front of my house. When I was not home, he took the large book shelf from the hall and replaced it with a small black pine version that now held some of my books and a few picture frames. Most of the books he boxed up and placed in the garage. There, he won my heart as he knew I loved black pine. He painted the sides and legs black on the pine kitchen butcher block. The house was beginning to look a bit different. There was a pile of discards he had placed on the patio to either donate or toss out of my life forever. It was hard as each item held a little story from where I had gotten it, or who had given it to me. I dug in the pile for old memories. Some things I gathered and brought back in. We had a tug of war with opinions and words. Some he won, some I won. The pile grew over time as the donation boxes filled. He smiled and I was hesitant to empty out a part of my life for good. I mulled it over, and he did not blink an eye. But, it was my house and he was a guest in search of a quest called "fix and save Mom."

Then, a week or so passed, I was home alone, and his words were fresh. I walked quietly and slowly through the rooms. Little memories brushing past as I walked in and out of years gone by. I could still hear his words, but remembered the years. I liked the small changes. The changes he had made brought newness in spite of my resistance. I held on to his words, but I hung on to my things at the same time. Even though I wanted to hang on to things, I could not help but think he was me about twenty-five years ago. I never collected things back then but I had gotten older and accumulated so much. Garage sales, thrift stores, and retail had been an entertainment and I was always in search of a unique find. Also, what had been given to me over the years represented the people and times in my life.

I walked to the kitchen window and peeked out through the lattice shelf to see the large beautiful backyard. Soft pink roses were still blooming in December, which he pointed out were overdo for trimming. A lemon tree ripe with its fruit and an apricot tree that promised white blossoms and apricot jam in the coming summer were glorious.

The lawn was scattered with small yellow leaves and green winter grass. I could hardly see it through the lattice. Well, maybe, I thought. I had to agree a rich view was hard to see for the clutter that blocked the window. A view that was always changing from the season before.

Down came the lattice and the shelf. It found a new home under the computer window facing the patio. A future home for a few potted red geraniums. After a few coats of white paint it looked brand new.

A quick trip to the department store brought jubilee red curtains for the kitchen window. I tied the centers back with ties and brought the garden in. I stepped back and loved the change.

I'd have to hurry if I planned to get things done before anyone returned home. Right there on the spot, I decided that maybe my old ways had not been the best ways; they were old and outdated. I was living in yesteryear.

I hurried and rearranged the living room working around the Christmas tree. I made a few trips to the garage. I removed item after item, refusing to think about the story of each piece. I did not care if Aunt Wilma or if Aunt Jane had given me a treasure years ago; they had thinned things out also. I was in a new moment and it felt kind of nice, kind of new.

I removed the green cabinet from the laundry room and put the contents where else, in the laundry room cabinets. It should not have taken a mental giant to figure that out. I'm sure Martha Stewart had advisors and help sometimes also, I'm sure of it.

Chris had gone from room to room giving me advice and ideas whether I wanted them or not. His words became inspiration for my change and my letting go. From his words new ideas generated. He was Mr. Martha Stewart and each one of us went on where the other left off. I had years behind me with old ideas and he had years ahead of him with new ideas; a division of our ages and era. But our experiences were related as we were from the same household.

In my excitement I removed items he had not even suggested. I opened the garbage can lid and tossed in knickknacks, colored bottles, and old ways of thinking. Each trip to the container made me feel lighter and more carefree. In doing so, I could see the treasures better that I decided to keep. The rooms began to open up. I even discovered a few things I had forgotten about. Jubilee red and soft yellow could live side by side.

He arrived home surprised and said, "See Mom, you have more room now; you can actually see what you do have; it's true, less is more, like they say."

We are always reinventing ourselves. I stepped back to view something he had learned somewhere in his youth. He had become the teacher and the parent. It was important that I let him have that role and that voice of development as I became the student, the child. I became refreshed and thought about change and what a good thing it is to be reminded of what we may have forgotten, what we may have lost. If *to teach is to learn twice,* then we both learned from one another through this project. We all have a voice, and when the time comes around, we need to let go, step back, and listen. We may just reinvent ourselves, others, and decorate our lives.

Little Jewels

Well, we fell into fall quite pleasantly. We have kids who mingle among us and the joy they bring changes our family forever. We rejoice and collect each memory as a treasure that allows each of us to become reinvented and renewed. The change is welcomed as it is that very purpose why we are who we are. What a beautiful time of year in our lives. The fallen leaves on brilliant, green grass and crispy, sharp clear days look new and we notice so much more. And the little people are known for the specialness one can never find somewhere else. How fortunate to be a part of the history of children in the making, and the natural formation of each one as they bridge a hole to their families, and what they do to enrich our lives.

Maisie helps me with yard work and she lessens my work load. Even though she is only eleven years old, she does a great job and is a pro with the rake. The mower is bigger than she is. Very carefully I supervise her closely and we trade off now and then. The other day she pushed hard to mow our small front yard. I could see it was not all that easy for her, but she pushed onward without complaints. She did an excellent job.

Shaking the bathroom rugs, taking out the trash, and putting dishes away has paid off for her. Those little things made her spirit and abilities push on to bigger things. She is proud of herself and I am proud of her also. I can give her a chore and when she is done, it's as if I had done it myself. We went from a grateful allowance to payroll.

Her mother started laying the foundation a few years ago when she was five going on six, by teaching her how to make her own sandwich. I thought she made a mess of things and my daughter Sara reminded me how she had to help me spring clean when she was Maisie's age. "It's all about independence and what we can do for ourselves," she said. "Don't you remember you had me doing things at an early age also?" What, the queen of chores is forgetting those years? Thank you, Maisie, for what you do around the house. Great job!

Then, there is Nicholas, a junior in high school, who must have been born doing homework to maintain his straight A's, and a star with his sports team and coach.

He has mowed the back lawn a few times for me, but his heart leans in the direction of school, school, and more school. He is always in and out at my house. It would spread him too thin to do chores at his own house, his other grandparent's house, and mine too. So I never ask him to mow the lawn or to do big things.

However, he loves my iced tea and our once-a-month biscuit and gravy; and he always attends our functions, even though he is very busy with school.

Then, we have little Chandler who only weighed one pound, six ounces when he was born. He fought for his life and won. Now, he is fifteen months, and I go to play and gather a joyous time, to my delight, of a child who makes everyone happy because he beat the odds and is so happy himself. It rubs off on all of us. His thirty pounds is solid and he is full of energy and play. While he is sitting on my lap, he will look at me, his little nose almost touching my cheek, as he waits and I linger, so I will not miss his darling anticipation for me to sing the patty-cake song. He is full of spirit and joy. Tears come to my eyes for such a priceless picture. And he does anticipate, and I wait, so I do not miss anything. Soft, flawless skin and the smell of baby mixed with his excitement over such a little common song. Patty-cake a baker's man, our clan, our little clan.

It's fall with winter wings as we watch our children sing. We are blessed, we are thankful.

As We Are

Everyone has something they struggle with. If you look at me, one would not guess my disability. I have bi-polar and with my meds, I require help around the edges. There are many out there like me with different or similar issues. To my joy, individuals I have encountered, their kindness, their smile or going out of their way, and what I do for myself refine those edges. The remainder, the entirety and the constant drip of dopamine, is up to me. It is my responsibility to take the meds on time, eat right, and get the right amount of rest. In doing so, and from the efforts of others, I gain positive effects.

I see other with disabilities, struggles, and situations they must cope with in this go around in life. And sometimes it can be a go around, not knowing if one is up or down or turned inside out. They should be honored because of their struggle to climb the mountain and speak softly in a world that is so loud. With our losses, torn relationships, illnesses, and hard cold facts we should honor one another.

People are awesome, and when I am alone, they come to my memory and I recall something someone said or did; something big or small. I have been uplifted by the smallest of small. Simple comments or conversations bring me to a better place and better state of mind. That alone encourages me to open my blinds in the morning and to reach. So many, just the way they are, have helped me cook or put a bow in my hair.

I am grateful to meet someone or I pull up my boot straps and walk into a crowd, hoping I blend in. Sometimes it is an unfamiliar crowd. It requires risk and bravery. I come out with confidence. Many times, others have been known, without their knowledge, to have been just what I needed for the day. Just the other day, a man and a woman who could not speak English crossed my path. We tried to communicate but we could not understand a single word the other spoke. But the heart and the experience was so notable it connected us in a priceless way.

In my travels, not ever do I want to forget the others: the ones who look normal. The ones whose situations and what they are going through give them a hard time just getting out of bed. I look in the mirror and I see them looking back at me. We are all pretty much the same. Everyone from the doctor, the policeman, the homeless, the car salesman, the waitress, and all those between, remind me how priceless life is and how special each and every one is, no matter how big or small.

I commend the stranger for taking the time, the teacher for believing, the irrigation man for waving as I drove past, the lady who said, "Welcome, come in," the homeless man for carrying a heavy box into the post office for me; and the lady in line for letting me go first, just because.

Thank you to all for pulling me out of the snow, for assisting me to have June in the winter and promoting me to wash the mud off my boots only to add glitter.

It is as we have heard: "It takes a village to raise a child." It also takes a village for us adults. After all, we are all grown-up kids.

Every once in awhile on a hard gloomy day, on a cold, stark winter's eve, I bump into a rainbow in the middle of the desert. I am grateful. It is monumental and distilled in my essence and documented for the day I truly need it. Some of us may not realize how valuable we really are; and the nice part is, when we help another, we also help ourselves.

The Next Chapter

Every Tuesday around midday, I grabbed my writing history bag and headed to the little bookstore on main street—The Next Chapter. A place that was ripe with atmosphere for some twenty stories and entries I wrote in a few months. I was thankful for a place that set the stage and encouraged us with all the books on the shelves and the smell and appearance of writers who had traveled down the same paths before us.

The class with all the wonderful comments and feedback, in addition to the guidance from our teacher, Marilyn Kregel, encouraged us to write more. The stories we heard from one another were not only full of life and creativity; they were little legacies.

We traveled to other countries and got a glimpse on the other side of the world; we visited old schoolyards, neighborhoods of long ago, and a family farmhouse. In descriptive words, we saw a movie made from an interview. We touched belongings and treasures of someone's grandmother, and we smelled fresh-baked Italian bread. We went to the fair in winter, and almost cried over the grandness of someone's grandfather. We listened and imagined grandchildren and relatives reading the stories years from now, and we smiled over their shoulders. We saw the night sky, early morning, and many characters. Our neighbors, sitting next to us, touched one another as we reminisced and heard of years gone by.

The luxury of hired help, the dedication of a tended rose garden was just as educational as "How I tried to live," and the medical terminology from someone who fought for her life. Our first house and daffodils brought gaiety. *Russian Gulch* read as if it were already published. We not only walked among the living, we walked among ghosts.

We were teachers, poets, and storytellers. We sprinkled history, a piece of our living legends, and everyday lives in a little book store, in the same manner as the published writers did with their works on the shelves. Fair thee well, keep recording, and keep embers in the ashes.

Vacation

"It looks like we are ready to go: it's hard to believe we have enough room with six adults, six kids, and two bloodhounds. I'll be sitting in the back so keep those dogs on their own side of the truck. Why did we have to bring them anyway?"

"We need them for watch dogs at camp. You'll be glad we brought them—you'll see."

"Gail, they're your dogs, you're used to them—I'm not. They're as big as horses. I can only imagine the food bill and I hope they are good for something . . . other than looks."

"Shu, we are going on vacation—calmly."

"Well, hope we didn't forget anything on our lists; if we have to stop at the store we will never hear the end of it. Just look at this stuff. You'd think we were going to camp for a year instead of two weeks."

"Well, Brenda, if we didn't bring it, we don't need it. Enough is enough and we are absolutely female—it's hilarious."

Gail yells to Bob that we are ready. The kids position themselves in their spots on the mattress and the truck, towing the jeep and the camping gear with the small boat on top, pulls slowly away from the familiar street.

"Gail, is the boat tied on good, is the jeep hooked on properly, this is scary."

"No wonder you had kids, it's in your personality to worry. Yes, Bob and George checked it all and they know what they are doing."

"Well, I've done so much packing I don't feel like I'm on vacation. Okay, I'll stop, but did it ever occur to you that we are doing something incredible? We must look like a calamity with all of us in the truck, the motorcycles, the kids, the dogs, the jeep, the camp gear, the boat, and all the things we really don't need. Okay, I'll stop; I'll close my eyes and tell me when we're there."

"Don't forget we're stopping at McDonalds."

"This is going to be an attraction, I know we are going to have a parking problem."

"Brenda, enough!"

"Sorry! Not another word, I promise—vacation, vacation"

"Once we are fishing from a trout stream in the mountains, you will love it."

"No kids standing up. Do you hear me?"

The kids nod and smile. No worries, just kid's stuff in the back of a truck headed for Mt. Lassen.

"Well Gail, I must say, the jeep doesn't sway, smooth ride."

"Of course, I told you all would be fine—how's my hair look?"

"Where we are going and how we are getting there in this open truck, I don't think it matters. But you look fine. Summery. Nice tan."

"Gail, I hate to bring this up, but look at all these people starring at us. Haven't they ever seen anyone going camping before?"

"Like you said, Brenda, we look like a calamity. That you are right on. But part of it has to do with your son sticking his tongue out at everyone."

"Stop that, we don't need a rude kid, we've got everything else."

"Mom, aren't you going to put on your sunglasses? You said everyone would be looking at us and they sure are. This is so funny. Gail, my mom didn't want you and Bob to bring the dogs, she said they'd be slobbering on everything."

"Ernie, mind your little business. I didn't say the dogs slobber."

"Yes you did, Mom—you know it."

"Well, your mom is right, but once we get to camp things will be better."

"Who wants what—burgers, fries, and cokes? Ernie wants two burgers, Chris, how many do you want?"

"Chris, Chris—where is Christopher? I thought he was in the front with you two guys."

"No, I thought he was in back with you."

"No one has gotten out of the truck, so I guess we left him at home."

"This could not be happening, bring the dogs and forget one of the kids. Must be a sign that we are not suppose to make this trip."

"Stop crying, Brenda, we'll find him."

"He is only five, I know he feels lost."

"Next trip will be a camper, or we don't go. My poor baby."

"Well, Mom, isn't he lost, Chris is lost."

"Ernie, your mom feels bad enough. He's not lost, we just left him at home."

The men do not waste any time getting back to the neighborhood. The truck rips down the streets, cars slowing down just to watch. Everyone's hair is flying in the wind.

"Oh my god! There he is on the front porch."

Brenda and George bail out of the truck and Chris is crying, rubbing the tears away, trying to be more than five years old.

"Christopher, where were you?"

"Down the street telling Jason goodbye. Why didn't you wait for me?"

"Honey, we thought you were in the truck. What are the police doing here?"

"Jason's mom called them. She said the police could tell you to come back and get me."

"Officer, all is okay, we forgot about this kid. All is well."

On the road at a slower pace.

"It's a wonder we don't get a police escort out of town. Wow, what a job! Gail, hand me that cooking sherry, I need a sip. A big sip. Do we have reservations?"

"It's first come, first serve."

"Mom, the sleeping bag is getting wet. The dog chewed a hole in the water jug. Mom, why is the dog raising his leg?"

"That's it; this is the last camping trip by way of insanity. Kids, can you say camper, camper, camper?"

"Mom, I'm still hungry. What does vacation mean?"

"I have no idea, ask your father."

"Wow, what a job."

Their Point of View

As we have heard, kids will be kids, and I prayed hard for miracles back in those days. It was a house full of kids and a dog on the run. Moments for me were rare, and holidays were comical with an open mind. The eighties were just as busy as the decade before and the decade after, especially with four kids and their friends. I can only imagine the clamor of an in-home day care. Miracles for me happened ever so often, and being the parent home during the day involved life of "No," "No," "No," "Can we go," "I don't want to go," and "I didn't do it."

Daily life involved four half-made beds made with a false heart, in a frantic rush out the front door by any one of the kids on any given morning. In early morning hours, all of their rooms came with attempts to lower the spreads to the floor in order to hide little things under the beds, along with crumpled sheets in little heaps tucked out of sight. Only a mother in search of truth always suspected them there.

Then there were the would-have-been-loyal vacuum cleaners that were constantly replaced. Of course, all the kids were innocent in the malfunction of the vacuum cleaner, as their father put in overtime with repair jobs that told the truth. Always something was lodged in the vacuum, with one of the kids standing limply, guilty and red faced, knowing he or she had not checked the carpet for small objects. The repair job always showed a foreign object that, according to the kids, just popped up out of nowhere. It was always someone else's fault. They were little criminals with alibis and age did not matter. The younger kids watched the older ones for tips and how things were done.

However, myself as the real trainer, I also worked overtime on laundry duty with vacuum in tow. I used Suave shampoo daily, on the kids' hair to keep it shiny and squeaky clean. I also gave Suave shampoo to the kids for quick fixes on bathroom fixtures if they needed extra chores or became under-house-arrest kid.

"Watch what I do, kids," I said as I picked up dirty laundry from the closet floor for the sole purpose of show and tell, and put in the hamper. It was decided if they were old enough to hide it, they were old enough to wash it. In addition, a few times the kids had to be loaded in the truck to retrieve clothes, the lawn mower, the family dog, and household items that were loaned out by a loan shark; who was a goodhearted kid that lived under our own roof. He would loan or sell anything to someone on an unfamiliar street on the other side of town. It was always a friend of a best friend that no one knew the name of.

Space meant nothing at our house. The kids were still under foot and insisted on functioning as if we all lived in one room. Daily necessities were often interrupted. Sometimes all of us had to grab our moments before time changed the clock.

"Can you give me some breathing room? I'm just going to take a bath."

"Joshua, leave your mother alone for a while."

"I just wanna see her."

"You see her every day," his father said.

"I wanna see her again."

As Joshua stood in the hallway by the bathroom door, Ernie flew up the stairs and didn't waste any words about his needs.

"Mom, please, one last time, then I'll learn how to do it. Please sew the button on my shirt. I'll mow the lawn without you asking; I'll do it all on my own."

"After my bath, can you wait?"

"The guys are on their way to pick me up. Please say you will."

"Joshie, go see your father, you don't need to stand outside the bathroom door; give me the shirt, Ernie."

"Mom, where are you going with my shirt?"

"I'll sew it in the bathroom before anyone else needs something; I need a break."

I shut the door, and Joshua knocked softly.

"How long you gonna be in there, Mom?"

I'll be out soon. Go do something seven-year-olds do, play with your roly-polie friends. Make dirt roads for you cars. Do something."

"I miss you," he whined.

"I'm not gone."

Sara joined Joshua at the bathroom door as he announced he was there first. Ernie came to get his shirt while a horn honked frantically in front of the house.

"Mom, will you French braid my hair? I'll dust and clean out the spoon drawer without you making a chore list for me."

I poked my head out the door and counted three kids standing in the hallway. "Where's your brother, he's missing? What does he need?"

Joshua beamed as he announced Chris climbed out his bedroom window to help deliver puppies down the street, and that we could keep one of them if I didn't mind.

"Ask your dad, he's in charge of that. Enough of this, go, just go. Be children somewhere else. I'm taking a bath."

"Do you want my bubbles, Mom?"

"No bubbles, go and play."

And play they did. They made little villages with little roads and little people made of wood, a remake of *Friday the 13th* while kids were being chased as they were running for their lives, and they made mini camp grounds complete with ponds and lakes and little fire pits with real fire. Hours of make believe.

The days passed slowly back then. It seemed at the time that it would all last forever, not so. The busy days were spontaneous and a surprise around every corner, including growing up and moving away. New chapters brought changes. We all changed, or we thought we did. Now, the kids are grown adults. Their needs were met, sometimes, in nontraditional ways. I laugh to myself thinking it was sheer delight, even on many days that were dysfunctional.

The kids are no longer my second set of steps, and they sew their own buttons, take quiet baths, often reflect and rekindle their earlier days.

So many times when they come to visit me, they are kids again. When I have had my time to myself, when the house seems empty and quiet, I start missing the old neighborhood and the joy of being needed.

I pick up the phone and dial one of the kids' numbers. No one is home; I'm disheartened. "Where is he?" I say aloud.

Finally, on the fourth number, Joshua answers, "Hello." I swallow slow and hard because now, after all this time, I need something, and I'm standing in the hallway waiting.

"Oh Mom, come on over."

I smile.

Sara

French braids and pigtails, blush and fluff. Two different temperaments: smudged nose, dirty jeans, frogs and tadpoles with lots of wiggly little things.

Miss Penelope the next. Primed in ribbons and bows, the scent of posies donned from head to toe.

When you please and only you decide, you'll be elegant and proper as you waltz your way to your world and lay your just so-so attitude on a field of flowers surrounded by shades of pink and hints of powder blues. "Yes, Mother dear—that is so lovely."

Dragging heals up the stairs, on this day, you hate climbing these horrid things; we should move—fluff, fluff.

The should-be-blue jeans are gray and the tennis shoes are somewhere between a has-been and a Saturday afternoon. Mother has become Mom and the sweatshirt says it all, "Dandelions are flowers too."

About the Author

1950-2012

Spending her childhood throughout Arizona and New Mexico, Brenda Montgomery developed an early passion for writing that she attributed to her family's travels. Brenda loved to share the beauty and the sorrow of everyday experiences through her art. Her wish was to create connections to other people's lives through the joy and purpose of her work, and to encourage creative responses from every life she was able to reach.

www.ingramcontent.com/pod-product-compliance
Lightning Source LLC
Chambersburg PA
CBHW061253170626
46809CB00007B/2981